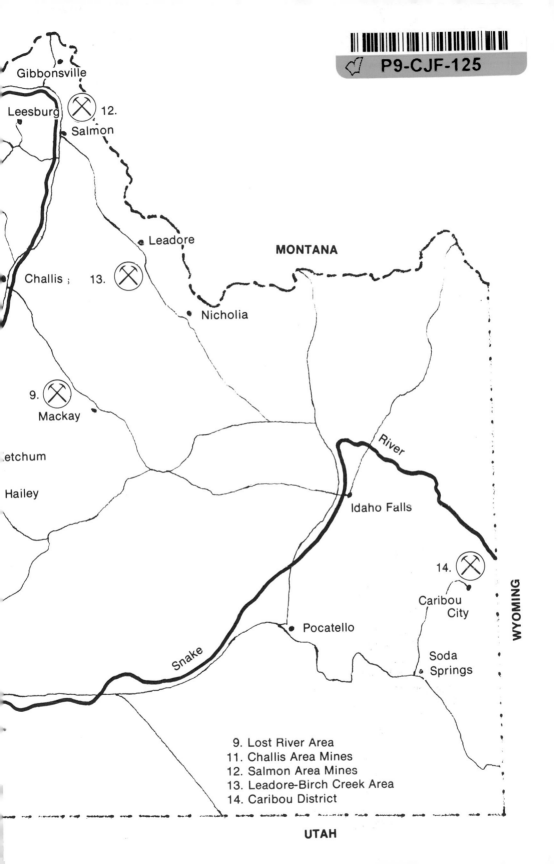

Gibbonsville

Leesburg ⊗ 12.
● Salmon

● Leadore

MONTANA

Challis ; 13. ⊗

● Nicholia

9. ⊗
Mackay

etchum

Hailey

River

Idaho Falls

14. ⊗

Caribou
City

● Pocatello

Soda
● Springs

Snake

WYOMING

9. Lost River Area
11. Challis Area Mines
12. Salmon Area Mines
13. Leadore-Birch Creek Area
14. Caribou District

UTAH

SOUTHERN IDAHO GHOST TOWNS

SOUTHERN IDAHO GHOST TOWNS

by

WAYNE C. SPARLING

The CAXTON PRINTERS, Ltd.
Caldwell, Idaho
1996

First printing February, 1974
Second printing September, 1976
Third printing May, 1981
Fourth printing September, 1989
Fifth printing October, 1996

© 1974 by
Wayne C. Sparling

Library of Congress Catalog Card No. 73-156484

International Standard Book Number 0-87004-229-7

Printed and bound in the United States of America by
The CAXTON PRINTERS, Ltd.
Caldwell, Idaho 83605
161785

TABLE OF CONTENTS

ACKNOWLEDGMENT

As with most articles having to do with history, it seems a necessity to rely on the words of authors from a prior age. Material for the brief historical sketches has thus been gleaned from the many historical volumes concerning early Idaho. Other information has come from many old-timers scattered about Idaho, and to these people I am very grateful. Many interesting hours have been spent talking about the early camps and mills and the events that took place. Once again I would like to express my appreciation to the many people who have so generously shared their knowledge of the early day miners.

Tim Williams, longtime prospector at Warrens, crushes ore in hand mortar before panning it for "colors."

INTRODUCTION

Discovering the assorted wonders of Idaho is very much like that small bit of knowledge that all of a sudden makes us realize what a great deal more there is to learn. Idaho is so large, so geographically diverse, and so abundantly endowed with natural beauty that to learn about a part of it only serves as encouragement to travel a bit farther or dig a little deeper. This book, therefore, has been prepared as a guide to acquaint vacationers and tourists with but one facet of a very fascinating state: the old mining camps.

Following in the footsteps of the fur trappers, the early gold seekers did much to explore Idaho and their mining camps helped to create a need for permanent communities. Within a few years after Captain E. D. Pierce's discovery of gold in northern Idaho in 1860, the miners' frantic search led them to establish camps as far south as the Owyhees and east to the Caribou Mountains. Some of the camps were merely tent cities, others consisted of a few log cabins, and still others, such as Iron Springs, became quite plush cities in their day. Yet scattered throughout such a vast wilderness though they were, they all played an important part. Each settlement or mine was named, each offered a new "diggings" to go to, and soon trails and wagon roads were built to accommodate the rush of prospectors. Communities soon sprang up around a mill or smelter and were as quickly deserted when the mine shut down. Many of the old camps, Doniphan for example, are completely gone, while others offer only the rotting remains of log cabins or perhaps stone foundations and scattered pieces of rusty tin. These old town sites have been included in hopes that they won't become completely forgotten.

The historic value of the old camps and mills is such that they should be shown every respect. They are a fragile reminder of Idaho's bonanza years and offer a tiny glimpse into the turbulent and troubled lives of our pioneer miners. Many of the old camps have been around for nearly a century; they show their age and they are fast losing out in their struggle to survive. In years past, various government agencies have been quick to destroy old buildings and settlements with scant recognition of their historic value. Heavy snows topple a few cabins each year, mills are torn down to recover scrap iron and quicksilver, and souvenir hunters add their share of destruction. Perhaps the one past event most influential in causing so many mills to be ravaged was the great scrap metal drive during World War Two. Most of the more accessible mills suffered during this time and particularly those throughout the Wood River area. In the more remote locations, the old stamp mills have managed to survive in better condition and thus offer more interesting subjects to photograph.

Photography is without a doubt the most rewarding way of recording your visit to an old settlement. The pictures, whether movies or slides, will refresh your memory for years to come, and all is left intact for others to see. As you visit the quiet solitude of an old mill, often located amidst rugged mountain splendor, it takes but little imagination to picture the bustle and activity of another time. Perhaps the miners are busy pushing loaded ore carts from the tunnel mouth, or as at numerous mills, a tramway with full buckets is busily coming down the mountainside. From the mill, clouds of steam and smoke arise, and throughout the valley echoes the steady roar of the stamp mill. Nearby, and usually not too far from water, a haphazard cluster of log cabins provide the necessary living quarters. Scattered throughout the timber, men are busy falling trees for mine timbers and cordwood for the boilers, while still others are digging the many miles of water ditches that were so necessary. Possibly this fascination with the lives of the early day miners is largely responsible for the interest people have in these old communities.

As most mining camps in Idaho were up in the mountains, July and August (and perhaps September) are the best months for a visit. Road conditions will vary from year to year and with the seasons. A good road one year may be completely washed out by the next spring runoff, so caution is urged on the more primitive roads. The main Salmon River as it crosses Idaho has often served as a north and south divider, and so it does with this book. All mining camps mentioned are located south of the river with the exception of three in the Salmon area. The pictures have all been taken in the past few years, and they are reasonably representative of what may still be seen. But even so, add another decade or two, the old logs crumble a little finer, the small towns grow a bit more modern, and the old camps will be only a few words on a page in Idaho History.

LIST OF ILLUSTRATIONS

SOUTHERN IDAHO GHOST TOWNS

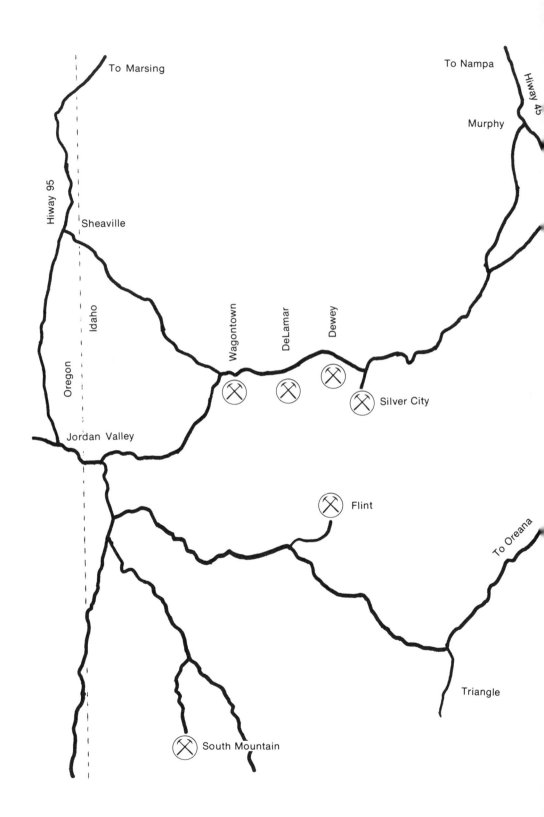

CHAPTER ONE

THE OWYHEE MINING AREA

After Michael Jordan's party of men discovered gold along Jordan Creek in 1863, the rush to the Owyhee mountains began. This group of prospectors had left Placerville with intentions of finding the lost Blue Bucket mine, but instead they uncovered one of Idaho's richest mineral lodes. At first the miners' activities were directed to the placers along the creek bottom, but further prospecting soon exposed rich ledges of silver and gold. As the untold wealth of these mines became apparent, efforts were made to connect this remote mountain area with the existing business centers. In 1864 a toll road was built from the mines by way of Reynolds Creek and John Fruit's Ferry (now Walters Ferry bridge) to Boise City, then a raw, young settlement started barely a year earlier. Various California merchants put up money to build a freight route so that they might share in this bonanza, and in 1866 the completion of the Silas Skinner toll road from Ruby City to Jordan Valley opened a route to the west.

Some of the mines were fabulously rich and generated intense rivalry and long, drawn out legal battles. Perhaps the most famous dispute was the shooting battle between the Ida Elmore and the Golden Chariot. Rather than wait for a legal settlement of their claim boundaries, the miners armed themselves, barricaded their mine buildings, and the fight was on. This affray lasted three days and cost the lives of several men before the U. S. Cavalry from Fort Boise arrived on March 28, 1868, and stopped the fighting. Even after the Cavalry had separated the miners, another argument and shooting in Silver City resulted in the deaths of two more men. One was Sam Lockhart, a mine owner, and the other was the prominent and well known J. Marion More, for whom Mores Creek was named.

Murphy is the county seat of Owyhee County and is about fifty miles south of Boise by road. A railroad was built into Murphy to haul supplies for the many mines in the Silver City area, but as the mining activity slowed, the railroad was used extensively by the livestock industry before being abandoned. Guffey was a small settlement along the railroad on the south side of the river near the mouth of Rabbit Creek. Today both the railroad and Guffey are gone, and only the bridge across the Snake River remains. Swan Falls Dam and powerplant was built to furnish electric power for the Trade Dollar and other mines. In 1901, a twenty-eight mile power line supplied electricity to Silver City, Flint, and Dewey. The museum in Murphy contains many interesting early day mementos and is sponsored by the Owyhee County Historical Society.

SILVER CITY

Silver City is without a doubt the queen of Idaho ghost towns. And while she may be a ghost town during the winter months, in the summer a combination of weekend visitors and local residents make for a busy community. The town contains many old and interesting buildings in various stages of disrepair as well as several nearby mine dumps. The Masonic building raises high above Jordan Creek, the upstairs of the old schoolhouse is a very interesting

Perched high on War Eagle Mountain, the Cumberland Mill near Silver City overlooks the Snake River Valley.

The picturesque Catholic church sits high on a rocky point in Silver City.

*The Stoddard Mansion in Silver City presents the ornate
"gingerbread" trim of its day.*

museum, and the once famous Idaho Hotel now stands forlorn. A
few of the buildings, notably the Stoddard House, have ornate
"gingerbread" trim, and some of the better houses now serve as
summer cabins.

Silver City had the distinction of having the first telegraph service in Idaho. In 1874, a line was built north from Winnemucca,
Nevada, and in 1875, the line was continued from Silver City on
to Boise City. Another first for Silver City was the printing of a
daily newspaper. In 1874, *The Idaho Avalanche*, edited by W. J. Hill
and considered one of the best papers in the West, became the first
daily newspaper in Idaho Territory. This newspaper, under several
different editors, continued to serve Owyhee County and in later
years the name was changed to *The Owyhee Avalanche*. Silver City
served as the county seat from 1867 until 1935, when it lost this
honor to Murphy.

The road from Murphy winds out over the sagebrush hills and
then up through the mountain mahogany and fir on New York
summit and on to Jordan Creek and Silver City. War Eagle and
Florida mountains are generously sprinkled with old mine dumps,
and narrow, steep roads wind every which way. The route from
Murphy to Silver City to DeLamar and on to Highway 95 and back
through Marsing makes a very interesting one day trip.

RUBY CITY - site

Ruby City, located along Jordan Creek about a mile below Silver City, was the earliest settlement in the upper valley. It was a boom town, born to serve the rich mines just being discovered, and it provided a headquarters for the rapid influx of miners. Ruby City could boast of being the first county seat of Owyhee County, but in 1867 these offices were moved up the creek to Silver City. As Silver City was laid out in a better location and was somewhat closer to the mines it soon took over and Ruby City began to decline. The better buildings were moved up to Silver City, and today there is virtually nothing to designate the site of Ruby City. From one place on the road the white stone markers in the Ruby City cemetery can be seen on a ridge against a background of junipers.

DEWEY

Continuing on down Jordan Creek, the next community was Dewey. A large cement powerplant building, just across Jordan Creek, and the mine dump behind it are all that remain today. Originally it was called Booneville, but after Colonel Dewey bought the mine in 1896 and rebuilt the town, including a magnificent three story hotel, it was renamed in his honor. With a new post office, a twenty stamp mill operating, and the prospects of being the terminus for the Boise, Nampa and Owyhee Railroad, it was a promising town. But within a few years the hotel burned down, and the decline in mining spelled the finish of Dewey.

DE LAMAR

De Lamar is next among the settlements along Jordan Creek. Named after Captain Joseph De Lamar, this town, along with so many other mining camps, was much larger than it appears today. Since the town site was located in a narrow creek bottom, the buildings were strung along both sides of the road and well up on the steep hillsides. The town was going strong in the 1890s: it had a red brick school, a newspaper, the *Nugget*, and the usual assortment of stores, liveries, and saloons. Many buildings have been moved away or burned down, but part of the old livery stable still stands, along with the largest and most impressive building, the boardinghouse. Mainly through efforts to recover any lost quicksilver, the mill is pretty much a pile of rubble. The cemetery is up on a steep hillside to the north of the road.

The power plant building is the only one left at Dewey.

Old boardinghouse at De Lamar with assay office in background.

WAGONTOWN - site

Wagontown was located along Jordan Creek where the road leaves the creek and continues on west to Highway 95. It was one of the stage stops on the road to Jordan Valley and at one time had several houses and a mill to rework the tailings that came down Jordan Creek from the De Lamar mill. Mines in the Wagontown area were the Webfoot, Last Chance, and the Garfield. The creek bottom was dredged in the 1930s so that outside of a few nearby mine diggings there is nothing left to mark the town site. The cemetery is about a quarter of a mile up a side road that leads off to the north.

FLINT

Flint is situated some ten miles southwest of Silver City and can no longer claim to be a ghost town. In 1966, the Bonnell family started to reopen the mine and are presently working to pump out the shaft and modernize the mill. There are several frame dwellings at Flint and part of the old mill is still standing. Formerly Flint boasted a post office, livery stable, stores and saloons, and a popula-

The old mill at Flint shows well constructed rock walls.

tion of fifteen hundred. Two remote graves on a juniper covered hilltop nearby are those of William L. Black and his daughter-in-law, Emma Myers. Indians were a constant threat to the early miners, and from a vantage point on Saddle Rock an Indian sped the fatal arrow as William Black stepped from his cabin. The Owyhee miners lost several prominent men in battles with the Indians before the U. S. Cavalry finally routed the Red Men.

SOUTH MOUNTAIN CITY

The community of South Mountain was located approximately twenty miles southeast of Jordan Valley, Oregon. Originally laid out in the early 1870s as Bullion City, the name was changed to South Mountain City upon establishment of a post office. It was one of the earliest mining camps in Owyhee County and for several years had the only smelter in Idaho. The district was made up of many mines, some of which were the Crown Point, the Golconda, the Bay State, and the Black Giant. In 1874, the South Mountain Consolidated Mining Company built a smelting furnace to process lead and silver from the nearby mines. Of the smelter only the black slag pile remains, and as some mining was resumed in the 1950s, the buildings are of fairly recent construction.

Wreckage of mill at South Mountain.

CHAPTER TWO

THE SNAKE RIVER AND THE SEVEN DEVILS

The mountains along the Snake River, from Weiser north to the Salmon River, have been well prospected over the years with many rich strikes being made. Probably the most important were the copper discoveries made in 1862 by a party of miners under Levi Allen.

This Seven Devils country, containing some of Idaho's most beautiful and spectacular scenery, has the origin of its name buried deep in legend. One story states simply that it was named by the early fur trappers for the seven high inaccessible peaks that dominate the skyline. But the prettiest legend concerns an Indian brave who became separated from his companions and wandered for days among these rocky pinnacles. Finally he grew weak and exhausted and began to have visions. At first there appeared only one devil, but as time passed, other devils came into view until he counted seven. Eventually the brave was reunited with his tribe and told them about his vision. In turn, the Indians related the story to the Hudson Bay trappers, and from then on these high peaks were known as the Seven Devils.

From Lockwood Saddle on past Towsley's Spring to Kinney Point and Sheep Rock, the ever changing views of the Snake River Canyon are truly magnificent. Al Towsley's cabin still stands, and while he tried a little mining nearby, perhaps his greatest claim to fame was that he wanted no door on his outhouse lest it interfere with his inspirational view of the canyon. From Ballards Landing on the Snake River to Helena high up in the peaks, winds the famous and steep Kleinschmidt Grade. Built with the idea of using steamships to haul ore up the river to the railroad, the dream quickly faded when it became apparent that the ships could not navigate upstream in the rough and rocky Snake River. The sternwheeler "Norma" was built to do this job at Huntington, Oregon, in 1891, but after a couple near-fatal trips she was successfully run on down

through Hells Canyon and used on the lower river. Transportation remained a problem for the Seven Devils miners and finally a railroad, the Pacific and Idaho Northern, was started from Weiser. By 1900 the railroad had reached Cambridge and eventually it went on to New Meadows, but because of the general decline in mining activity, it never reached the mines it had started for.

MINERAL CITY

Situated in the southern part of the mountains, Mineral City lies in a rather remote valley that empties into the Snake River. The initial discovery was made in 1880 by John James and Jim Peck, and the mines were the Silver Bell, the Hancock, the Black Maria, and the Black Hawk. Several small smelters were brought in, and farther down the valley some rusting machinery and a glistening black slag pile marks the site of one. The town had a store, hotel, three saloons, a livery, and several houses, but today only a few buildings remain and they are strung out down the creek bottom. The road in by way of Fourth of July Creek is good to the summit, but down the Snake River side it is narrow and steep, much better suited for four-wheel drive outfits. That is, if you plan to return the same way.

Only a few cabins remain at Landore but a peak population of a thousand called for many more.

HEATH and RUTHBURG - sites

Along Brownlee Creek, the settlements of Ruthburg and Heath sprang up. Silver was discovered in 1875 by Jim Ruth and Tom Heath, and they freighted in a small stamp mill to grind their ore. Ruthburg was located about a mile up Camp Creek, and today the site has only the rock foundation of the old stamp mill and a few small mine dumps. Heath, with a post office, was the larger community and was situated on the East Fork of Brownlee Creek, a short ways upstream from Brownlee Guard Station. The Railroad Mine was the largest producer and a smelter was installed. During World War Two the smelter was junked out, the cabins have been demolished, and today only a wooden oil bunker for the smelter and the slag pile are left to indicate this townsite.

CUPRUM

Cuprum, the Latin word for copper, was at its peak of activity in 1898. In 1897 the establishment of a post office and the construction of a hospital to care for injured miners had gotten the town

Ore carts were used in the mines at Mineral.

Wooden oil bunker is sole remnant at Heath. The smelter was just below this bunker along the road.

off to a rousing start. The mines up Indian Creek were going strong, a railroad was being built out from Weiser, and a smelter was being erected. So confident were the mine owners that the Seven Devils copper would develop into a rival for Butte, Montana, that they started construction on a railroad grade along the side of White Monument. Needless to say, this great excitement died down in a few years and the railroad never reached the mines, but the white scar of the old roadbed can still be seen on the hillside above Towsley's Spring. Cuprum is still quite active during the summer months, with loggers and summer cabin owners taking the place of bearded miners.

As a mining town, Cuprum saw its greatest activity in 1898.

HELENA

Originally known as the Town of the Seven Devils, Helena was renamed by a party of miners from Montana. The mines were the Helena, the White Monument, and the Peacock, so named for the beautiful blue coloration in the copper ore. Nestled at the upper end of twenty-two mile long Kleinschmidt Grade, Helena was granted a post office in 1890. The breathtaking view from Kinney Point plus the magnificent mountain scenery along the road make a visit to Helena into a memorable event. There are still several log buildings that remain and others in various stages of decay.

LANDORE, DECORAH (site) and GARNET TOWN

Landore was born in 1898 when T. G. Jones located a claim near the Arkansas Mine and had it plotted into lots. The town quickly prospered, a daily stage left for Council, and a weekly newspaper was printed. In 1904 a smelter was built, but this venture did not prove successful. Today the tall brick chimney from this smelter is the most noticeable feature at Landore. A few old cabins are

Cabins in Helena are not far from the Peacock mine.

still standing, and to have boasted a population of a thousand there must have been many more. Mines along Indian Creek were the Blue Jacket, the Queen, the Bitter Pill, and the Alaska. One half mile on down Indian Creek is the town site of Decorah, a very beautiful name for what reportedly was the fun town for the miners from Landore and Helena. Just a short ways up Garnet Creek from Decorah was the three cabin settlement of Garnet Town. The tumbled remains of these cabins are still there. Farther up Garnet Creek was the famous Blue Jacket mine and its accompanying cluster of cabins.

PLACER BASIN

Although rich float ore had been picked up in Placer Basin since the 1890s, it was not until the early 1930s that Tom Williams, with a prospectors one last try, uncovered the long sought-after ledge. The jubilant partners soon sold out, and the new owners built the mill that stands today. This mill was in operation in 1935 and 1936 and reportedly took out over three million in free milling gold. The skeleton of the mill is still standing but the other buildings are

This tall chimney served the mill at Landore.

This mill in Placer Basin accounted for better than three
million in gold.

pretty much a pile of splintered lumber. The road to Smith Mountain
and Black Lake passes right through Placer Basin.

BLACK LAKE TOWN - site

In its rugged mountain setting, Black Lake is one of Idaho's
most beautiful lakes accessible by road. During springtime, the drive
in is equally scenic: the slopes of Smith Mountain are blue-purple
with wild lupines, and last winters snow banks along Devils Dive
add to the many rushing streams. With numerous lakes and streams
edged by lovely campsites, the entire Seven Devils has a rich variety
to offer the vacationer.

The mining at Black Lake is quite interesting in that the mine
tunnel is located high above the lake, and the ore was carried by
a cable tramway clear across the lake and on down to the mill.
The climb up to the mine is well worth the effort, and following
the tram towers leads to an awe-inspiring view of the lake. As the
mine and mill were quite a ways apart, a large boardinghouse for
the miners was built up near the mine. Heavy snows have long
ago turned this and nearby buildings into a pile of debris. While

visiting this area above the lake, our attention was attracted to a rusty brown ore cart at the mouth of a tunnel. A closer inspection with binoculars turned the "ore cart" into a huge old buck enjoying the cool shade of the tunnel. Another time at Helena a sudden commotion in one of the cabins announced the abrupt departure of a small deer. So at least the old miners efforts aren't being completely wasted.

The huge mill below Black Lake was scrapped out during World War Two and the remains burned. Today only some foundation walls, rusty tin, and burned timbers are left.

From the amount of broken glass on a large rock along the road, it would appear that every tippler in Black Lake Town took the utmost delight in shattering his bottle. The sight of so much broken glass is enough to make a bottle collector want to cry a little. Black Lake Town was built along the creeks below the mill site and these buildings were also burned. Nothing at all remains.

IRON SPRINGS and PARADISE

A visit to the old community of Iron Springs calls for a hike

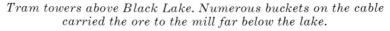

Tram towers above Black Lake. Numerous buckets on the cable carried the ore to the mill far below the lake.

of about five miles. An old wagon road led to these towns, so following the trail isn't too difficult. From the lack of mining evidence around Iron Springs it would appear that the old Iron Springs Mining Company was more interested in mining the stockholders pockets than in mining their placer claims. The Company also operated a large sawmill and many rotting piles of sawed lumber still remain.

With electric power, some twenty-five or thirty houses, a hotel, saloons, stores, a livery stable, and other buildings, Iron Springs was quite a fancy settlement, especially when you consider its remoteness and accompanying transportation problems. About a half mile below Iron Springs, on the flats along Paradise Creek, was the sister community, or perhaps suburb, of Paradise. All of the buildings in Paradise, except one, have been flattened by snow and weather. Several buildings in Iron Springs are still standing, but most are in various stages of falling apart.

RANKINS MILL

Approximately six miles by trail, on past Iron Springs, is the mining camp of Rankins Mill. The broken remains of an old wagon

This building, well insulated with sawdust, was used for cold storage at Iron Springs.

Wagon wheels offer proof of a road into Rankins Mill.

are evidence that a wagon road existed, but in places it has eroded away to barely a trail. Tracks for ore carts and cave-in tunnel entrances show that some mining was attempted. The large mill has been flattened into a shapeless pile of weathered boards with the ore crusher resting on top. A few buildings remain, but they are losing out in their struggle with the elements. Just above the mill, a cluster of five or six small cabins served as living quarters for the miners.

BOISE BASIN

When the party of men under Moses Splawn and George Grimes discovered gold on Grimes Creek in 1862, the stampede to Boise Basin began. This vast basin was one of the major discoveries of the gold rush years, and people flocked in from all directions. Towards the end of 1863 there were estimates of twenty thousand people scattered through-out the hills. One of the principal routes was by boat from Portland to Wallula or Umatilla, then overland to the Washoe Ferry on the Snake River, up the Payette River to Horseshoe Bend, and over the hill to the Basin. This three hundred mile trail from Umatilla to Placerville took approximately thirteen weary days to travel. The trails were later widened into wagon roads and the Harris Creek road from Horseshoe Bend to Placerville was originally built as a toll road.

The Boise Basin area includes Mores Creek, Elk Creek, Grimes Creek, Ophir Creek, and Granite Creek, and the communities of Idaho City, Centerville, Pioneerville, Placerville, and Quartzburg. A tribute to its richness is that mining continued up through the depression years, with some spots of activity at present. Boise Basin mining was predominately some form of placer operation; that is, some method of washing the gravel and separating the gold particles was used. Since placer mining requires a water supply, it is said that considerable gold remains where it is located higher than a ditch could be run. So bring along your gold pan and try your luck.

IDAHO CITY

Idaho City is one famous mining camp that has refused to die and instead has prospered into the thriving community that it is today. During its early years it was known as Bannock City or West Bannock to differentiate between Bannock, Montana, since at that time both towns were in Idaho Territory. In 1863, Idaho

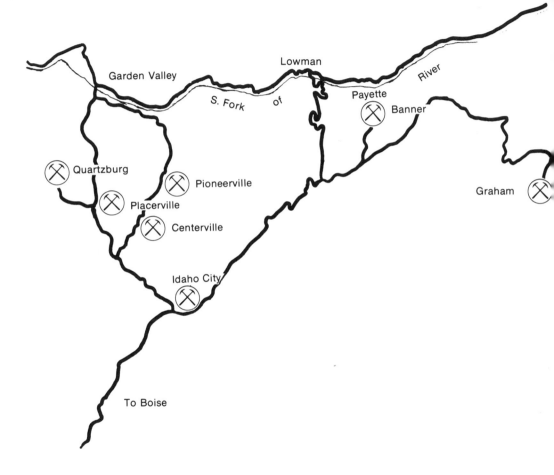

Boise Basin miners were enlightened by the "Idaho World" for over fifty years.

City had a population of six thousand and was being seriously considered for the territorial capital. It lost out, however, and in 1864 the territorial capital was moved to Boise City from Lewiston. This was quite an honor for the fledgling city of Boise, considering that its townsite had only been laid out the year before. With the printing of *The Boise News* in 1863, Idaho City could at least boast it had a newspaper a year earlier than Boise. *The Boise News* was later changed to *The Idaho World*.

The immediate area around Idaho City has been extensively placer mined and dredge tailings can be seen for miles along Mores Creek. Even the buildings in town were raised up on pilings so the ground underneath could be mined. When water was available for sluice boxes the miners worked day and night, often by the light of huge bonfires or pitch holders. Up Elk Creek, just north of town, are large gravel bars washed out by hydraulic giants from the hills behind. Giants were the ultimate in placer mining, for the high pressure stream of water could flush away an entire hill to get at the gold bearing layer of gravel.

A stamp mill, a machine used by the early miners to crush ore, has been set up in Idaho City so that visitors can see it in operation. These mills came in various sizes from one stamp to as high as fifty stamps, but usually as a battery of five stamps. It is interesting that in 1898, the Boise Iron and Reduction Works (forerunner of the Baxter Foundry) advertised a one stamp mill with a two hundred pound stamp to sell for one hundred dollars. Or for one hundred fifteen dollars you could get the same mill with a three hundred pound stamp.

Despite several disastrous fires, such as one in 1865 that destroyed about four-fifths of the town, including the newly completed Forrest Theatre, Idaho City still has several interesting old buildings. Among these are the Court House with its iron shutters and wide veranda (formerly the Orchard Hotel), the historic Catholic Church, the old Masonic Hall, and the Boise Basin Museum building. Under a protective cover are the log remains of Idaho's Territorial Prison. No visit to Idaho City would be complete without a side trip to Boot Hill Cemetery, with its intricate iron fences and intriguing headboards that tell tales of murders, shootings, and hangings. Pine covered hills surround Idaho City, and with numerous campgrounds nearby, it provides a good headquarters only a short drive away from the other Basin communities.

CENTERVILLE - site

Known as the prettiest of the basin towns, Centerville was located on Grimes Creek at the mouth of Slaughterhouse Gulch. This is near the point of initial discovery by the Grimes party. During its hey-day Centerville had a population of three thousand, a hotel, saloons, express office, stores, and houses, but today only the trash of old buildings is left to mark this site. Just across Grimes Creek to the east are the scant remains of the old Twin Sisters Mill. From Centerville the old stage roads led to each of the other Basin communities, with a mail stage running up to Pioneerville as late as 1914. About a half mile to the west, on the old road to Placerville, are the town's two graveyards. The Protestant cemetery is on a hill south of the road and the Catholic cemetery is up on a hill to the north.

PIONEERVILLE

Pioneerville, Pioneer City, or Hogem: they are one and the same place. The story of the name of Hogem is that the first miners in the area hogged up all the good placer ground. As the next group of prospectors became quite irate over this greediness, they let forth a few appropriate words and moved on down Grimes Creek to start Centerville. Human nature being what it is, it is interesting to note

*Stamp mill set up in Idaho City for the "Gold Rush Days"
celebration.*

*Remains of early arrastra in Placerville. By dragging heavy
stones around and around, the ore was ground up so that
the gold could be separated.*

that in the White Pine Mining District in Nevada there was another
Hogem, named under very similar circumstances.

Only a few buildings remain at Pioneerville, but it was once
a fair sized community with a population of two thousand and the
first post office in the Basin. All along Grimes Creek you can see
the rock piles and scars left by placer mining operations. After
the original miners with their gold pans, rockers, and sluice boxes
got through, along came the deeper-reaching dredges, leaving their
characteristic tailings piles. Grimes Dam and powerplant on the
South Fork of the Payette River were built to supply electric power
for the dredges and mining settlements. On past Pioneerville at
Grimes Summit is a monument to mark the grave of George Grimes,
who was killed by Indians while on the initial prospecting trip and
hastily buried near this spot.

PLACERVILLE

Situated on one of the main roads into the Basin, Placerville
became a supply base and grew rapidly. In 1863 the town had a

Remains of the Mammoth Mill on upper Grimes Creek near Pioneerville.

population of five thousand and some three hundred houses. Many old buildings, including the Magnolia Saloon, still remain, but the town is gradually building up with summer cabins.

A simple marker in the Placerville Cemetery denotes the grave of the three fiddlers. These wandering musicians made a living providing entertainment in the remote camps, but in Placerville their luck ran out. Actually there were only two musicians, Fred Cursons and L. Moulton, and the third man was a miner carrying a considerable amount of gold dust. The miner, George Wilson, was the intended victim of the robbery while the musicians were killed only to insure their silence. This slaying took place in June of 1865 while the trio was walking from Placerville to Centerville. These brutal murders created a wide-spread furor, and a few days later the authorities arrested John Williams, by reputation a gun slinger and gambler. In spite of a near lynching at the time of arrest, a verdict of not guilty was handed down by the District Court a month later. No one else was ever apprehended, and the true identity of the murderer remains lost in the mists of time.

Although Williams went scot-free on this charge, the Idaho Courts decided to set an example and drive this breed of badman from the Basin. Accordingly, Williams was indicted on another charge; this time for robbing John Carpenter of two hundred dollars in September of 1863. In this case, lawyers Merritt and Ainslie elected to use a most bizarre form of defense. When Congress passed the Organic Act of the Territory of Idaho on March 4, 1863, it was found to contain no criminal code, and without laws there were no crimes to be guilty of. This oversight was rectified in February of 1864, when the Territorial Legislature passed the Criminal Practices Act. Since the robbery that Williams was accused of occurred during this eleven month absence of criminal laws, he once again won his freedom. This odd chain of events, starting with an unsolved triple murder, at least brought publicity to a little known mistake made during the formation of Idaho Territory.

QUARTZBURG

The placer miners soon turned to quartz mining, and in 1864 the first stamp mill was set up on Granite Creek by W. W. Raymond. This same year saw the beginning of development work on the Gold Hill claim, a mine that was to become one of the largest producers and create the settlement of Quartzburg. The Gold Hill had a twenty-five stamp mill and was in operation for many years. In 1931 a disastrous forest fire swept through the Basin, and the mill and all the buildings in Quartzburg, except one, were burned. This lone building, which was the post office and store, and the tailings piles along the creek are all that remain.

In those pioneer days it didn't require much activity to earn a name for each location, and Boise Basin had many of these small, obscure settlements that have been long forgotten. Buena Vista Bar, a community across Elk Creek from Idaho City (towards the air strip), was probably the largest and best known. Just below Idaho City and along the banks of Mores Creek was Moorstown. On up Mores Creek near the mouth of Pine Creek was the village of Pine Grove. Between Idaho City and Centerville was the tiny camp of Pomona. At the junction of Granite Creek and Grimes Creek stood the town of Boston. Between Placerville and Quartzburg the miners along Granite Creek had their Granite City.

With so many prospectors in the area , nearly every creek and gulch has an old cabin or maybe the dugouts lived in by the Chinese miners. Roads throughout Boise Basin are usually very good and a visit to these old placer camps makes a very interesting Sunday drive.

The post office was the only building to escape the forest fire that destroyed Quartzburg in 1931.

This cabin is said to be the old saloon at Banner.

BANNER and EUREKA - site

While Banner and Graham are not in the Boise Basin they were discovered by miners traveling and prospecting from the Basin area. James Hawley and Jess Bradford discovered the Banner lode in 1864 while searching for a better route to Rocky Bar. They soon sold out to an Idaho City merchant by the name of Crafts, and he had a mill freighted in from Kansas City. This mill was a twenty stamp Fraser and Chalmers, with a cable tramway to bring the ore down from the mile long tunnel. Of all the rich mines scattered throughout the Basin, the Banner was the only big producer of silver, turning out well over three million dollars in silver bullion. The Elmira Silver Mining Company ran a steady operation for many years, and with a first class post office, Banner was an important community on the road north from Idaho City. The old mill site is still identifiable and a few cabins remain. Eureka was a small camp just below Banner that failed to develop.

GRAHAM

Excitement ran high in 1885 when Matt Graham told of finding

Tram towers were built to carry the ore down from Silver Mountain.

wide veins of ore high on Silver Mountain. In 1887 a tunnel was driven and a fifteen thousand dollar road was completed, and by 1888 the boom was at its peak. But Graham proved to be a mining town built more on fiction than fact. After the town and mill had been built at considerable expense to the stockholders, it was discovered that there just wasn't sufficient ore to make it pay. The mill ran only eight or ten hours and never ran again. With no jobs and winter coming on, the people hurriedly packed up and left Graham, with the luckier ones finding work at the Banner Mill. This venture was financed with British money and millwrights were brought over from England to build the large mill. The mines are up on Silver Mountain behind the mill and a long tramway was built to haul in the ore. Some of the wooden tram towers are still standing, well supported by trees that have grown much taller. The rotting remains of many old cabins are scattered throughout the trees on either side of the mill. Although the road into Graham winds through some beautiful mountain scenery, it is only open during the summer months and then it is better suited to travel by pickup.

CHAPTER FOUR

WARRENS and the MARSHALL LAKE DISTRICT

Discovered by a party of miners from Florence, who were prospecting south of the Salmon River, the Warrens placers were well known for many years. The rush to Warrens' diggings nearly depopulated the northern camps, and as the newcomers spread out they soon found gold in Pony Meadows, in Ruby Meadows, and along the slopes of War Eagle Mountain. The original trail into Warrens was quite steep, so a new one was built that started up French Creek and across the head of Fall Creek and down Lake Creek to the Warm Springs (now Burgdorf), then along the Secesh and over the ridge to Steamboat Creek and down to Warrens. This new trail was ten miles longer, but the grade was much easier for the pack animals so it became the popular route.

Named after Jim Marshall, a pioneer trapper and miner, the Marshall Lake mines were a much later discovery that resulted from the rush to Thunder Mountain. These mines are pretty much stair-stepped down along Bear Creek and the country is quite steep.

WARRENS

Preceded by Pierce, Oro Fino, Elk City, and Florence, Warrens is the fifth oldest mining community in the state. Although James Warren is credited with the original gold discovery in 1862, the first settlement was not named after him but instead was called Richmond. The first building, quickly erected to protect a pack train load of goods, was a crudely built log house at the mouth of Slaughter Creek and around this sprang up the village of Richmond. Richmond, of course, was named after the Confederate Capital by Southern sympathizers. With the intense feelings prevailing in those Civil War days, the unionist miners moved on down the creek a mile and started the settlement of Washington. Unfortunately for Richmond, it was located on good placer ground, and in 1866 the

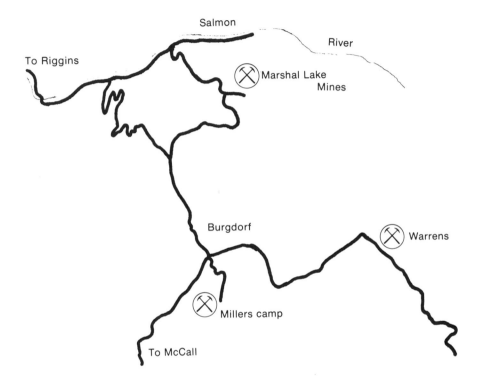

Salmon

River

To Riggins

Marshal Lake
Mines

Burgdorf

Warrens

Millers camp

To McCall

buildings were removed and the property was mined. Washington continued to grow, and in 1869 it became the county seat of Idaho County, taking this honor away from a declining Florence. In turn, Washington lost the county seat to Mount Idaho in 1875, and about this time the name Washington dropped from use and Warrens came into popular acceptance.

Like most of Idaho's mining camps Warrens had its share of Chinese miners, with nearly a thousand living in the area at one time. One account states that in 1880 Warrens had six hundred Orientals with their own store, saloon, gambling house, and butcher shop. With the completion of the transcontinental railroad in 1869 at Promontory Point, Utah, thousands of Chinese laborers were left jobless and many drifted north to the mining camps in Idaho. As the Chinese traveled about looking for work, usually in groups for mutual protection, they suffered severe discrimination at the hands of the miners. They were scarcely regarded as human beings, some camps passed regulations prohibiting the entrance of any Orientals, other times they were robbed or shot with but the slightest provocation, and in 1864 the Territorial Legislature passed a tax of four dollars a month on alien miners. Aside from the effects of slowing down the Chinese rush to the placer fields, the tax was an important source of revenue for the young territory.

The Rescue Mill was an early producer at Warrens.

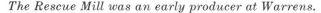

*Still busy during the summer months, Warrens was once
home to nearly a thousand Chinese.*

Yet as much as the white miner despised the Chinese, he was
always willing to make the last few dollars on a worn out claim
by selling it to them. The Orientals only rarely worked any virgin
placer ground or staked a new claim, for to do so would invoke
instant and drastic reprisals from neighboring white miners. So
the Chinese mining companies were usually confined to reworking
old placer claims, and by long hours of hard work they made it
pay. Each community usually had a Chinese laundry, they worked
as cooks and house servants, and performed the menial tasks about
town, such as carrying water and firewood. Through their quiet
industriousness, they gradually were accepted and in later years
became well respected community members.

After the individual miner was through, dredges worked their
way along Warrens Creek, leaving their inevitable rocky wasteland.
The extent of the dredge tailings below Warrens is enormous; literally the entire valley floor has been turned upside down. Over this
vast rockpile the rusting remains of one old dredge still stands
guard. Very popular during the summer months, Warrens still
shows a strong spark of life.

MILLERS CAMP - site

Built on a ridge just above Ruby Creek, Millers Camp (also known as Ruby City) was the settlement for the miners along Ruby Meadows. Forest fires have long ago cleaned this area, so nothing remains of the original cabins. In more recent years, attempts were made to dredge Ruby Meadows and the dredge still remains.

BURGDORF

While not a mining camp, Burgdorf Hot Springs was well known to miners at Warrens and Marshall Lake. Known simply as "Warm Springs" to the earliest travelers this favorite stopping place next was called "Resort" with a post office being established in 1903, during the Thunder Mountain rush. Fritz Burgdorf saw the advantages in these natural hot springs, and in 1870 he secured a deed to the property and built a hotel and way station. Fritz and Jeanette Burgdorf were a hospitable couple, and their hotel served as a social gathering place for parties and during the holidays. Built during later years, the present hotel with its rustic native furniture is

*Dredge in Ruby Meadows is follow up to original placer
miners from Millers Camp.*

virtually a museum. The name "Resort" was gradually dropped and about 1914 "Burgdorf" came into general usage.

MARSHALL LAKE MINES

While the Marshall Lake District had many scattered mines, no settlements developed to serve the whole area. The Golden Anchor Mine with its many buildings and a schoolhouse served as the local headquarters. The Kimberly Mine and its small beautiful lake is uppermost, then the Sherman Howe, and still lower is the Golden Anchor, which was discovered in 1915. J. A. Czizek, an early day Inspector of Mines for the State of Idaho, was at one time the owner of the Golden Anchor properties. With the reopening of the mine in 1940, a post office was established under the name Czizek. When World War Two forced the closing of so many mines in 1942, Czizek folded up, with many of the miners moving to Stibnite. On White Creek, along the road in, is the remains of a power plant built to furnish electricity for the Sherman Howe Mine.

Far below the mines on a ridge above Bear Creek, the tent town of Bungville appeared in 1902. This short-lived settlement was composed of miners from Florence, who were waiting for the heavy snows to go off so they could begin prospecting. Some were also

Rustic wooden furniture creates veritable museum of hotel at Burgdorf.

waiting for the trails to open up, so they could continue on to Thunder Mountain. Roads in the Marshall Lake district are rough and steep, so visitors should at least be equipped with a pickup.

Steep ground requires tall buildings at the Golden Anchor.

To Warrens

River

Werdenhoff
Mill

S. Fork of Salmon

Sunday Mine
Moscow Mine

Big Creek

To McCall

Yellowpine

Roosevelt

Dewey and
Sunnyside Mines

To Landmark

Stibnite

CHAPTER FIVE

THUNDER MOUNTAIN — BIG CREEK AREA

Because of the remoteness of this region, prospecting and mining occurred slightly later than for the rest of Idaho. About 1900, stories of the Caswell brothers' gold discoveries on Monumental Creek began to circulate and Colonel William H. Dewey (of Owyhee County fame) became interested. In the fall of 1901, Colonel Dewey declared his faith in Thunder Mountain by purchasing the Caswell claims for one hundred thousand dollars. This act immediately raised everyone's gold fever to a high pitch, and the last of Idaho's great stampedes was under way. Thousands of poorly equipped people, both on foot and on horseback, traveled this rough, inaccessible country with only visions of easy gold to lighten their load.

Interest in Thunder Mountain ran high in the spring of 1902 with stage lines being planned, a telephone line under construction, and the Union Pacific searching out the best route for their rails. Since the mines were accessible only by trail, it was natural that a wagon road be planned and local newspapers avidly pursued the merits of each route. While roads from Boise and Garden Valley were eventually completed, it was Colonel Dewey's wagon road from Emmett to Roosevelt that carried most of the freight. The Idaho Northern Railroad, owned by Colonel Dewey, ran from Nampa to Emmett, and by starting his road at this railhead, he hoped to promote business for the railroad. From Emmett this wagon road led up through Brownlee and High Valley, across the Payette River at Smiths Ferry, then on through Long Valley to the small outfitting community of Thunder City. At Thunder City the road turned eastward over Big Creek Summit to the popular way station at Knox, then rose sharply over Cabin Creek Summit and down Johnson Creek to Twin Bridges. Climbing again to Trapper's Flat the road wound down and across Riordan Creek, only to climb up over Monumental Summit and down the long grade into Roosevelt. Parts of this tortuous old road have been utilized in the present road system,

*Located near Profile Summit, the Red Metals Mine was going
strong in the early 1900s.*

and other portions can still be covered with a pickup or four-wheel
drive vehicle.

The rush to Thunder Mountain at least served to open up the
great back country in central Idaho, a beautiful area of clear, swift
streams and deep valleys surrounded by high, rock-strewn peaks.

BIG CREEK

Today, Yellowpine is the jumping off point for the Big Creek
and Thunder Mountain areas. A favorable location, coupled with
a reasonably light snowfall, made Yellowpine a natural site for
a settlement, and for years a genial Mr. Behne operated the store
and post office. When the road from Yellowpine to Edwardsburg
was completed in 1933, it was a great boon to the miners and
ranchers along Big Creek. The Edwards ranch, with a post office
under the name of Edwardsburg, served the remote Big Creek country for many years. The Edwardses were Southern aristocracy who
migrated north during the later years of the mining rush and took
up a homestead near the mouth of Logan Creek. While Mrs. Edwards
ran the post office, Mr. Edwards became interested in the mining

game, holding claims at Copper Camp and for a time operating the Sunday and Moscow mines on Logan Creek.

At the very head of Big Creek, the Cleveland Mine dates from prior discoveries in 1885, when the Alton district was struggling to make itself known. Near Profile Summit, the Red Metals Mine and the Wilson Mine share opposite sides of a ridge, and Profile Sam Wilson became a well-known figure. Placer mining down in the meadows along Big Creek was undertaken by the Golden Placer Mining Company. A short ways up from the mouth of Smith Creek is the old camp of the Smith Creek Hydraulic Mining Company, farther on is the huge mill at the Werdenhoff Mine, and at the head of Smith Creek is the Independence Mine, located in 1898. Ramey Ridge, the Golden Hand, Copper Camp, and the Snowshoe Mine were all names familiar to the miners along Big Creek.

Big Creek Store and Big Creek Ranger Station are now the centers of activity for the valley. The road in from Yellowpine is good as far down Big Creek as the mouth of Smith Creek. Beyond there it gets very rough and narrow, possibly the most miserable road Idaho has to offer. Another road leads from Big Creek to Warrens so that a loop drive can be made from Yellowpine to Big Creek,

A few miles below Elk Summit on the South Fork side stands the Smokehouse Cabin. Pioneer mail carrier Curly Brewer built this cabin as a refuge against the severe winter storms.

up over Elk Summit and down across the South Fork of the Salmon River to Warrens and back out to McCall. Elk Summit, where alpine flowers still bloom in August, affords a panoramic view of Idaho's intriguing back country. Past Elk Summit the descent into the South Fork seems almost unending; long before you reach the valley floor, you'll swear there's an odor of brimstone in the air. Finally the road does level off a bit and crosses the river on a good steel bridge, only to begin the long climb back up through the fragrant pines to Warrens.

STIBNITE

Discovered during the Thunder Mountain rush, the mines around Stibnite became famous for mercury, antimony, gold, and tungsten. The Meadow Creek Mine was one of the first discoveries, and all of the early mines were opened up by tunneling. It wasn't until the World War Two mining effort that the huge open pit was created. During the war years this mine became a leading producer of vital tungsten, and the town of Stibnite was at the peak of its glory. Changes in metal stockpiling procedures following the war years led to the closing of the mine, and the huge mill has been

Recreation hall was once center of activity for Stibnite.

dismantled into a pile of debris. Most of the houses have been trucked out over the hazardous road to McCall and sold. The glory hole complete with its small lake and running stream can be seen far below the road that leads into town.

From Yellowpine the road to Stibnite follows up along the East Fork of the South Fork of the Salmon River. After passing through Stibnite the road climbs up over Monumental Summit and then follows down along Monumental Creek to Roosevelt Lake.

ROOSEVELT

Colonel Dewey's display of confidence in the Thunder Mountain mines immediately triggered a great influx of people, and in 1902 the town of Roosevelt was established. Named for Teddy Roosevelt, the townsite was laid out by The Idaho Land and Loan Company of Boise and lots were sold for $100 on up. The town was strung out along Monumental Creek with the Dewey Mine just two miles away on Mule Creek. Although there were attempts to establish other towns, a good central location plus the opening of a post office in July of 1902 helped Roosevelt become the leading community.

Logs from the old cabins still float on Roosevelt Lake.

From a blossoming tent village it had grown to a substantial town by 1904, when the wagon road and telephone line were completed. Over this new wagon road came heavy mill equipment for the Belleco mine, and construction of this mill on Marble Creek, along with a steady output from the Dewey Mill, made for prosperous times.

Upon acquiring the Caswell claims, Colonel Dewey had a sectionalized ten stamp mill and a steam boiler packed in on horses. This mill ran more or less continuously from 1902 until 1907 and produced the biggest share of gold mined on Thunder Mountain. Over the ridge east of the Dewey Mine, the Sunnyside claims were purchased by a group of Pittsburgh industrialists who established The Belle of Thunder Mountain Mining and Milling Company. The forty stamp Belleco Mill on Marble Creek had a mile and a half long tramway that carried the ore down from the ridge. This elaborate operation got under way in 1905, and after a series of problems, including the lack of proper equipment to separate the gold and the growing reluctance of the stockholders, the mill ran again briefly in 1906, never to run again. A large portion of the tunneling at the Dewey Mine collapsed in 1906, and with the remaining ore becoming steadily poorer in grade, the Dewey Mill closed down in 1907. Although several small mining ventures continued to operate the failure of the two largest companies heralded the finish of Idaho's much publicized Thunder Mountain.

Aside from the closing of the mines, the death of Roosevelt was enacted in a more dramatic way. On the last day in May of 1909, a huge mud slide let loose in a draw just south of the Dewey Mine and started flowing down Mule Creek. The sodden earth didn't travel any faster than a man could walk, but it inexorably moved boulders and trees and when it finally stopped, after about thirty-six hours, Monumental Creek had been effectively dammed. Only about twenty or thirty people still resided in the town, and as the water slowly came higher they hurriedly moved possessions to higher ground. Still, there wasn't time to remove everything, and for years people came to "fish" for items they could salvage. Today the lower shore of Roosevelt Lake is covered with logs that have floated up from the old cabins, and when the water is calm you can see the shapes and outlines of buildings.

The present Sunnyside Mill is a later development, having been constructed during the winter of 1924 and 1925. Like the Belleco, it is located on the Marble Creek side of the ridge, and a short tramway was built to bring down the ore.

*Tram towers supported the mile-and-a-half-long cables that
brought the ore down to the Belleco Mill.*

Sunnyside Mill was built during the winter of 1924 and 1925.

THUNDER MOUNTAIN CITY

In March of 1902 several Weiser businessmen purchased a group of placer claims at the mouth of the West Fork of Monumental Creek and set up the Thunder Mountain Placer Mining Company, Ltd. This townsite was named Thunder Mountain City, and with five mercantile stores, a blacksmith, an assay office, a hotel, restaurant, and nine whiskey mills, it was Roosevelt's closest rival. Some prospects were discovered on nearby creeks but nothing big developed, and Thunder Mountain City served mainly as a stopping place for the many travelers on Monumental Creek.

The similarity in the names Thunder City and Thunder Mountain City has created some confusion and warrants an explanation. Thunder City was located approximately six miles south of Cascade and served as a way station and outfitting point on the wagon road into the mines. When the railroad came up the Payette River and established the station at Cascade in 1913, it doomed the small villages of Thunder City and Crawford. Although Thunder City was still going in 1916, no trace remains today.

Venable Mill featured steam-powered Chilean ore crusher.

Thunder Mountain City was situated about three miles on down Monumental Creek from Roosevelt. This town was deliberately laid out as a money making enterprise, and lots were sold for one hundred dollars and up. The tumbled remains of several log buildings can still be seen, and the numerous leveled-off spots were used for tent houses.

Marble City was another log and tent town on upper Marble Creek, below the Sunnyside Mine. This town was used mainly by people coming in from Salmon, Challis, and Ketchum. Only trails came in from this direction, and after crossing the Middle Fork of the Salmon River, the travelers would take the trail up along Marble Creek, crossing the ridge at the head of the creek to get on to the Dewey Mine and Roosevelt. Marble City was in existence only a short time, and there are no remains.

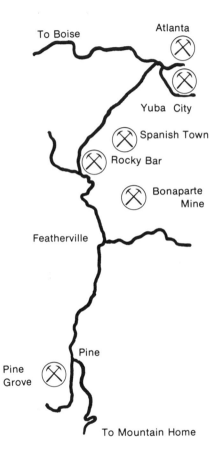

CHAPTER SIX

ROCKY BAR and ATLANTA

The discovery of gold on the Feather River in 1863 touched off a new rush to what became known as the South Boise diggings. As the miners spread out in their search, camps were set up on Red Warrior Creek, Elk Creek, Bear Creek, and Cayuse Creek. Because of the remoteness of the district, mining methods were necessarily crude and many arrastras were built. A toll road was completed in 1864, and freight wagons started to roll in from the railhead at Kelton, Utah. From Mountain Home the toll road led to Dixie, Pine Grove, Junction Bar, and finally to Rocky Bar.

The Atlanta mines were not discovered by miners from the South Boise, but they were found by a party of miners from Warrens. The mines near Atlanta suffered even more from the lack of transportation until a road was built over the mountains from Rocky Bar. This original road went up across Elk Creek, then along Boiler Grade Creek and over Bald Mountain and down Camp Gulch to the Yuba River. Years later the present road over James Creek Summit was built.

ROCKY BAR

With the largest mines nearby on Bear Creek, Rocky Bar quickly became the leading settlement for the South Boise miners. In 1864, with a population of nearly twenty-five hundred, it became the county seat of Alturas County. And along with Idaho City, Rocky Bar was a contender for the site of the territorial capital. When Alturas County was created in 1864, the first Territorial Legislature designated Esmeralda as the County seat. But since Esmeralda wasn't much of a village and Rocky Bar was starting to boom, the county officials quietly moved their office up to Rocky Bar. This honor was held by Rocky Bar until 1881, when Hailey won the election and became the seat of Alturas County.

The exact site of Esmeralda is shadowed in doubt. Locations vary from below Featherville to the area across the Feather River east of Featherville and all the way up to Red Warrior Creek. If Esmeralda was a placer camp along the Feather River, the dredging that took place in the 1920s would have removed any traces. The most convincing source, however, states that Esmeralda was a cluster of four or five log cabins located on the north side of the Boise River below the mouth of the Feather River and about halfway between Featherville and the Jackson Bridge. When the rich placer beds were opened up near Rocky Bar, these prospectors quickly moved out, and the cabins in Esmeralda were left to rot away.

Quartz milling got under way with the use of arrastras, and by 1864 there were fifty-three arrastras working in the South Boise area. An arrastra grinds up the mineral bearing ore by simply dragging four heavy grinding stones around and around over a floor of other rocks that fit snugly together. They are quite slow, but they have an advantage in that they can be made entirely of native materials, just wood and rocks. Most were powered by a wooden, hand-built water wheel, but a few were operated by a horse or mule walking in a circle. It is regrettable that there are so few remains of arrastras to be seen.

Metropolis of Rocky Bar retained the Alturas County seat for over seventeen years.

Old cabin along the Feather River. Bellows was necessary for blacksmith work.

Later on, when freight roads were built, several stamp mills were brought in, the largest being the fifty stamp mill at the Elmore Mine. Stamp mills were a considerable improvement over the arrastras in that a much greater tonnage of ore could be processed with better control over the fineness. One account states that a twelve stamp mill was hauled by ox team from Omaha to Rocky Bar for thirty cents a pound. In 1892 much of Rocky Bar was wiped out by fire, but the town was soon rebuilt and mining continued. A large Chinese settlement hugged the banks along Steel Creek. There are still a few summer residents in town and one cafe and bar. (Or should we say saloon?) The old mills have pretty much been torn down. With the death of Charley Sprittles, Rocky Bar's last winter-time resident, the deep snows and wintry winds have this old camp all to themselves.

HAPPY CAMP - site

Named appropriately, Happy Camp was the scene of the initial gold discovery and so became the first of the South Boise camps. This placer camp was on the Feather River, approximately two miles below the confluence of Bear Creek and Elk Creek. Both sides of the Feather River throughout this area are well scarred up with old placer diggings. Like so many other camps, the placers at Happy Camp last supported a settlement of Chinese, who reworked the rocky tailings. Of the camp itself, only foundation hollows and bits of trash remain.

SPANISH TOWN

While not a town in the strictest sense of the word, Spanish Town was the name given to the mining settlement on Elk Creek near the mouth of the East Fork of Elk Creek. And like so many old camps, it was a much larger operation than would appear from the remains.

Mine tunnels have caved in and eroded away, buildings have fallen to the elements, and iron from the old mill has been hauled away. When the miners first prospected up Elk Creek, they discovered old arrastras and other evidence that early Spaniards or Mexicans had preceded them. Hence the name Spanish Town. A few tumbled buildings remain at Spanish Town and scattered along Elk Creek are several log cabins and other remnants from mining operations. The old road along Elk Creek is so washed out that you quickly end up walking, probably right down the creek bed or back and forth across it many times.

PINE GROVE

Located on the road between Dixie and Featherville, this settlement had a log hotel and restaurant and several houses. Discovered in 1888, the Franklin Mine was the largest and most profitable, while some of the other mines were the Boise, the Columbia, and the Mountain View. The completion of Anderson Ranch Dam and the resulting backwaters placed Pine Grove under some twenty feet of water. A few of the buildings were moved upstream to the present village of Pine, while others were moved to higher ground near the Franklin Mine. The old mill for the Franklin Mine was situated near the high water line, and it was completely dismantled. Ore bins and mine dumps can still be seen back against the hillside.

ATLANTA

Discovered in 1864, the mines near Atlanta proved to be very rich and added to the excitement already created by the rush up the South Boise. Located on the Middle Fork of the Boise River,

Camshaft from stamp mill at Spanish Town.

Ore bin for the Franklin Mine at Pine Grove. The site of this village is buried under the backwaters of Anderson Ranch Dam.

The jail in Atlanta was conveniently located over a small creek.

the extreme distance from existing business centers was a serious drawback. Only steep mountain trails existed, until completion of a wagon road to Rocky Bar permitted mills to be freighted in for the quartz miners. The Buffalo Mine and mill was one of the earliest, and other mines were the Pettit, the Last Chance, the Tahoma, the Lenora, and the Monarch. Mining continued on into the later 1930s, and some work is presently going on.

Whether fact or fantasy, the Chinese in Atlanta are credited with the naming of Greylock, the high mountain just north of town. The mountain presents mostly gray rock to the viewer, so the name Greyrock would seem appropriate. But the Chinese custom of substituting l's for r's, and the miners' quickness to accept slang or popular words, has resulted in the name "Greylock," which is still used today. The town still has many residents, and with several campgrounds and good fishing nearby, it entertains numerous summertime visitors.

YUBA CITY - site

Situated up the Yuba River and just below the mouth of Decker Creek, Yuba City was on the old road from Rocky Bar to Atlanta.

The Talache Mill, one of Atlanta's later producers.

*Mine workings at the Minerva mine on Decker Creek
near Yuba City.*

On up Decker Creek is the old Minerva Mine and mill and the remains of several other mine buildings. Nothing is left of Yuba City, except a few building outlines and one well-built stone foundation.

There were a few other camps in the area that have long since disappeared. Alturas City was a tiny settlement at the mouth of the Yuba River. Brownstown was an obscure camp up the Little Queens River. China Basin was a camp of Chinese placer miners on the north side of the Boise River. Back on the Rocky Bar side of the mountains, the Bonaparte Mine and mill on Cayuse Creek supported quite a settlement. And a short distance up the Feather River from Featherville, a few cabins and a saloon made Junction Bar. A map printed in 1894 clearly shows Junction Bar, Rocky Bar, and Atlanta but no sign of Featherville.

CHAPTER SEVEN

THE WOOD RIVER MINES

Extending from Highway 68 on the south to Galena Summit on the north, the hills along both sides of Wood River are liberally sprinkled with mine diggings. After the cessation of Indian hostilities in 1879, the miners began to scour the Wood River area in earnest. West of Hailey, nearly every gulch has its group of mines. There were camps up Deer Creek, in Greenhorn Gulch, up the East Fork, over the hills in Elkhorn Gulch, and along Lake Creek. As the reduction of lead and silver required a smelter, there were smelters built at Bellevue, near Hailey at the mouth of Indian Creek, at Ketchum, at Galena, and across the Little Wood River at Muldoon. The Wood River mines were so important that the Oregon Short Line hurriedly extended its tracks up the valley to better serve the area.

The Triumph Mine, up the East Fork of Wood River, was in full production during World War Two, but since then it has been largely dismantled and hauled away. Of all the many old mines and mills that flourished, there is little left to see. At several mill sites only the rock foundations are left, and of some settlements there is no trace at all. For those more deeply interested in history, the Blaine County Museum in Hailey contains many interesting articles associated with early day miners.

BELLEVUE and BROADFORD

The present town of Bellevue is located on Highway 93, and about a mile to the west and across Wood River is the old settlement of Broadford. At first named Jacobs City in honor of Frank W. Jacobs, and renamed in 1880, the town of Broadford grew up to serve the needs of the Minnie Moore and the Queen of the Hills mines. In 1884 it had a population of six hundred. These early mines were very rich and did much to promote other mine discoveries

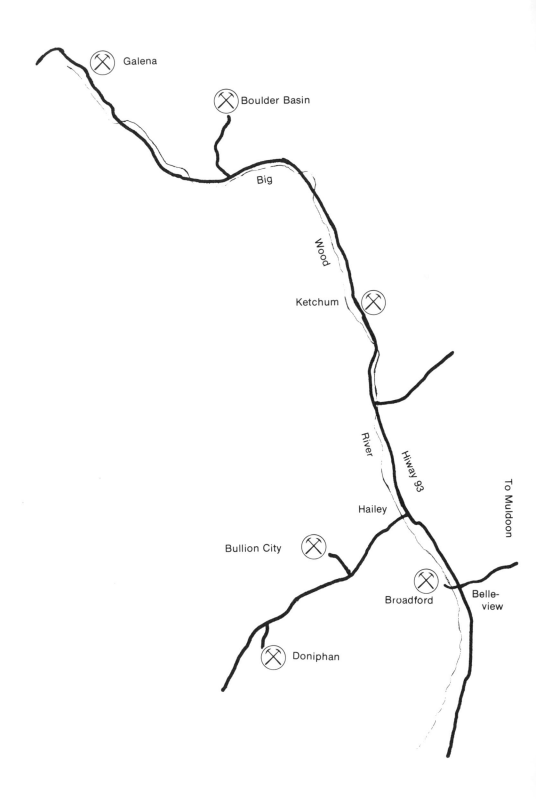

Galena

Boulder Basin

Big

Wood

Ketchum

River

Hiway 93

Hailey

To Muldoon

Bullion City

Broadford

Belle-
view

Doniphan

in the area. As newer buildings have spread out from Bellevue, the old settlement of Broadford has been gradually absorbed by the present community.

MULDOON

To the east of Bellevue, across Little Wood River and up on Muldoon Creek, was the early settlement of Muldoon, named after a champion wrestler of the day. Born in 1881 to service the silver mines up Muldoon and Argosy Creeks, the town had a peak population of fifteen hundred people but only lasted a half dozen years. It was a fair sized town as mining camps go and had all the usual buildings of its day; livery stables, saloons, stores, houses, and a hotel. A smelter was built nearby and twenty-three charcoal kilns to furnish it with fuel. In 1887 the smelter was sold at a Sheriff's sale, and this spelled the finish for Muldoon. Today only a black slag pile and the remains of the kilns are left.

Charcoal kilns are sole evidence of mining industry that created Muldoon.

*Doniphan was located just a short way down the valley
from these ruins of the Big Camas Mill.*

DONIPHAN - site

Started during the 1880s, Doniphan flourished for twenty years,
yet today so little remains that diligent searching is necessary to
find any indication of a town. Fires have raced over this sagebrush
country and pretty well cleaned up the remains of any buildings.
Located approximately fifteen miles southwest of Hailey, Doniphan
served the mines in the Hailey Gold Belt. These were the Big Camas
and the Tip Top, both of which had mills, and the Hidden Treasure
and the Black Cinder. The Big Camas and the Black Cinder were
recorded in 1865, the earliest mines in what is now Blaine County.
The town had a post office, store, houses, a schoolhouse, and the
usual saloons.

BULLION CITY - site

Situated about seven miles west of Hailey, Bullion City in 1882
had a population of seven hundred. Some of the mines were the
Mayflower, Bullion, Jay Gould, May Queen, and Idahoan. These
mines were very rich and contributed much to the growth and pros-

perity of Hailey. Hailey was a raw, young town in 1881, but a favorable location, with many mines nearby and a railroad on the way, soon brought it into prominence. In a hotly contested fight for the Alturas County seat in 1881 Hailey won out over Rocky Bar, Ketchum and its closest rival, Bellevue. When Alturas County was split up and Blaine County created in 1895, Hailey retained the county offices. While Hailey thrived, Bullion City declined until the post office was discontinued in 1890. Outside of a few nearby mine dumps, there is nothing left in this narrow gulch that once was home to a goodly number of miners and their families.

KETCHUM

Once known as Leadville, Ketchum is one old mining town that has skyrocketed into prominence as a nationally known recreation center. During its mining days Ketchum had a newspaper, *The Ketchum Keystone*, a post office and about one hundred businesses. A toll road wound up Trail Creek and connected Ketchum with the other mining settlements of Clayton, Bayhorse, and Custer. Up Warm Springs Creek led a road to the many mines on Boyle Mountain, while at the mouth of the creek, The Philadelphia Mining and Smelting Company had the largest mill in Idaho. This mill ran on water power from Wood River, and had four tall stacks, electric power, and twenty kilns to feed it with charcoal. It was closed down in 1893. The completion of the Oregon Short Line Railroad into Ketchum in 1884 brought an end to the twenty mule team freight outfits that had supplied the Wood River Valley for so many years.

BOULDER BASIN

Jagged rock ridges, tumbling white water, and clear alpine lakes mark Boulder Basin as one of the truly rugged and scenic spots in Idaho. There are several old cabins scattered around the basin and the old mill at the Golden Glow Mine. High up on the rocky ridges around the basin can be seen the tunnels and diggings of the early miners. The rough terrain and heavy mill equipment must have been a real challenge for the freight wagons. Some of the mines at Boulder were the Ophir, Trapper, Tip Top, Bazouk, and Sullivan. The road in is passable by jeep only, but the sheer beauty of the basin makes the trip well worth the effort.

GALENA - site

The town of Galena dates from 1879 and was the earliest mining community on Big Wood River. Situated at the mouth of Gladiator Creek, it served the Senate, Gladiator, and other mines. It had a population of about eight hundred, a post office, restaurant, livery, hotel, houses, stores, saloons, and a smelter located on Senate Creek. The town site is approximately where the Galena Store is today.

Wood River also had some other small and obscure mining camps. Gillman City was west of Hailey near the mouth of Bullion Gulch. Up the East Fork of Wood River was North Star, East Fork City, and fartherest up was the community at the Mascot diggings. West of Ketchum, over Dollarhide Summit, was Carrietown. Also west across Dollarhide are the placer fields and other mines up Little Smoky Creek. With an abundance of beautiful mountain scenery, numerous campgrounds, and fine fishing streams, Wood River valley has long been known as an outdoorsman's paradise.

Only a jeep road leads up to Boulder Basin and the Golden Glow Mill.

A modern gold washing machine on Little Smoky Creek.

Miners in Boulder Basin enjoyed some of Idaho's ruggedest alpine scenery.

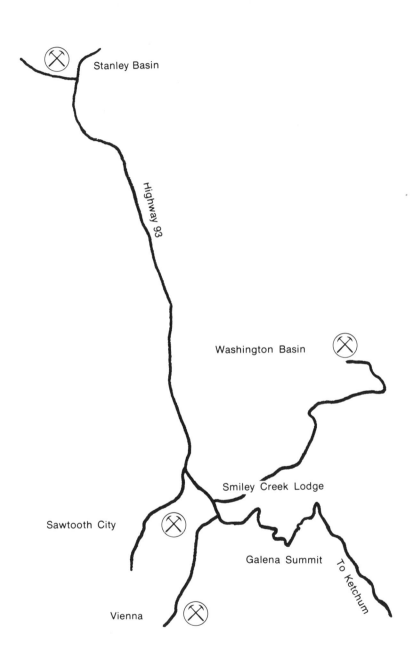

Stanley Basin

Highway 93

Washington Basin

Smiley Creek Lodge

Sawtooth City

Galena Summit

To Ketchum

Vienna

CHAPTER EIGHT

SAWTOOTH VALLEY

When Levi Smiley discovered silver at the head of Smiley Creek in 1878, he touched off the mining activity that created the towns of Vienna and Sawtooth City. The mines were strung along a high ridge at the head of three drainages: Smiley Creek, Beaver Creek, and Alturas Lake Creek. Only Lake Creek failed to develop its own town. Located north of Galena Summit on the headwaters of the Salmon River, these early camps enjoyed some of Idaho's finest scenery.

VIENNA — site

Vienna was the largest town and was in existence from 1879 to 1892. It had a population in excess of eight hundred, nearly two hundred buildings, and in 1882 a weekly newspaper, *The Vienna Reporter*, was printed. A toll road to Ketchum was completed in 1880, and two mills were built, one mill being a duplicate of the General Custer Mill. The mines and mill buildings are farther up on the ridge from the town site, and at present some mining is being carried on. As early as 1914, it is reported that all the buildings in Vienna were reduced to mere piles of timber. Today there is only a little rubble left, and a Forest Service sign designates the townsite.

SAWTOOTH CITY

Sawtooth City, located on Beaver Creek, grew out of additional mineral discoveries to the north of the Vienna Mine. The city had some twenty-five houses, a population close to six hundred, and lasted until 1889. A pack trail led over the mountains and down Mattingly Creek to the Boise River, so that ore could be packed over to the mills near Atlanta. This, of course, was before any mills were built in Sawtooth Valley. Later, in 1883, the Columbia and Beaver Company built the twenty stamp Columbia mill a short way above the town. The well-laid stone foundations of the mill still remain. Well braced by pines, only one old cabin remains in Sawtooth City, but the crumbling remains of many others are scattered out among the trees.

WASHINGTON BASIN

The numerous mines and beautiful mountain scenery combine to make this high basin worthy of a visit. With timberline nearby and small blue lakes surrounded by sheer rocky ridges, the landscape is some of Idaho's prettiest. There are several old log cabins scattered about the basin and the wreckage of a mill. You can't help but marvel at the great amount of work accomplished by the early freighters in bringing in heavy boilers over such rough country. The road into the basin is at best a pickup road and at worst a four-wheel drive vehicle would be necessary.

No story of Washington Basin would be complete without mention of George Washington Blackman, the Negro miner. He accompanied a group of miners in prospecting the basin in 1879, and for many years after, he worked claims on Fourth of July Creek and in the basin. When the snows got deep, he would head south, but

Trees help support the only remaining cabin in Sawtooth City.

Cement arrastra in Washington Basin has stood up well over the years.

Old boardinghouse at the Vienna Mine.

*Heavy boilers in remote Washington Basin presented a real
challenge to the early freighters.*

each spring he came back to Ketchum to wait for the trails to open
up. Visitors were always welcome at his cabin, and he was well
respected by his fellow miners. He worked at the Redbird Mine
in later years and is buried in the cemetery at Clayton.

STANLEY BASIN

When a party of prospectors from Warrens discovered gold up
a tributary of the Salmon River in 1863, they named the basin
in honor of their oldest member, a Captain John Stanley. Other
placers were soon discovered on Big Casino Creek, Rough Creek,
Kelly's Gulch, Joe's Gulch, and Stanley Creek, which was later
dredged. Word of the discovery soon got around, and in 1864 there
were about two hundred men working the creeks around Stanley.
The tattered remains of a stamp mill up in Joe's Gulch is proof
that some quartz mining was attempted. Today, as you drive along
the picturesque Salmon River near Stanley, there is little to show

Although placer mining was predominate near Stanley, this old mill in Joe's Gulch shows that some lode mining took place.

from the old miners' activities and only by taking the side roads and searching around can you find the old cabins and hand piled rocks of the placer miners.

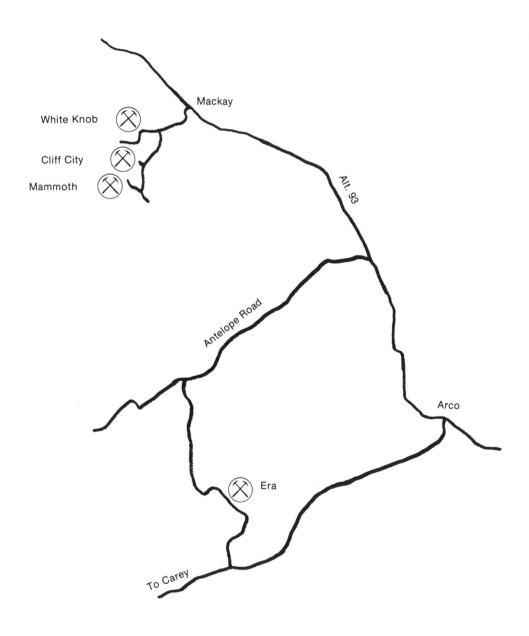

White Knob

Cliff City

Mammoth

Mackay

Alt. 93

Antelope Road

Arco

Era

To Carey

CHAPTER NINE

LOST RIVER MINES

Mineral discoveries were made in the White Knob Mountains as early as 1879, but settlements did not spring up until 1884, when the first boom got under way. The headwaters of Cliff Creek saw the development of Cliff City, while down in the valley Houston grew into a supply center for the area. The mines were predominately copper, and with typical early day enthusiasm, they were envisioned as a rival for Butte, Montana. Apparently, dreams of approaching Butte's fabulous production record are latent in every struggling copper camp. Later activities did produce quantities of copper, however, and from 1900 until the 1930s, the Mackay mines were the leading copper producers in Idaho.

Houston started as a stage station on the freight route from Blackfoot to Challis. From a single store owned by Joe Gallagher, it grew into a settlement of some seventy buildings with a population of two hundred. When the railroad was built up the valley in 1901, and the town of Mackay laid out, it sounded the finish of Houston. Gradually the people and businesses moved up to Mackay, and nothing remains except the cemetery.

John W. Mackay was manager of the White Knob Mining Company in 1900, and it was through his efforts that the Oregon Short Line brought its tracks up Lost River Valley and platted the townsite. In making up the plans for Mackay, the town's civic leaders inserted a paragraph prohibiting the building of saloons and bawdy houses. But the rough and tumble miners had come in from Montana where whiskey and wild women were a way of life, and they were not about to abandon their pleasures. Consequently, they went a mile north of town and built up their own cluster of saloons and sporting houses. Another village of the same character was constructed south of Mackay, and hourly a horse drawn bus traveled between these two cities of sin. After watching this easy money go back and forth for two years, the businessmen in Mackay relented and a red light district with adjoining saloons soon appeared. With several unsolved shootings to its credit, this rough, little mining town of seventy years ago bears little resemblance to the quiet, respectable community of the present.

CLIFF CITY

Big Copper was the name of the mine responsible for the growth of Cliff City and the construction of a two-stack, fifty ton smelter. This mine was on the south side of the mountain, and the lively camp along Cliff Creek was home to nearly three hundred miners. The smelter ran only a few years, however, and dreams of a copper empire began to fade away. Today rock foundations of the huge mill and rusting parts of the smelters are mainly what is left. Of the many cabins there is scant evidence. Perhaps there is a leveled off spot littered with pieces of a broken stove, or you might find a pile of rocks used as a hearth, along with scattered bits of tin and glass. A visit to Cliff City calls for a hike of about a mile, but the trail isn't too steep or difficult, although it does cross a snowslide area.

Cliff City had the first smelter on White Knob Mountain.

WHITE KNOB

The White Knob Mine was discovered in 1900 by a man named Darlington, and he immediately sold out to Mackay. Darlington then gave up the mining game, and taking his money, he went farther down the valley and established the small railroad settlement of Darlington. This new mine was on the east face of the mountain, and the village of White Knob quickly sprang up. Along with a wonderful view out over the valley, this town soon had a store, post office, boarding house, school, saloon, and even a theatre. Several old cabins still stand, but most of the buildings have been completely demolished.

Other large scale developments that produced millions of dollars worth of copper took place in the early 1900s. A large, electric powered tramway was built from Mackay up to the ore bins on White Knob Mountain, and on the west side of Mackay a smelter complete with two large blast furnaces was erected. The Empire railroad built a narrow gauge track that wound up the mountainside for nearly eight miles before reaching the mines. This railroad used two, twenty-three ton, Shay mountain-climbing locomotives and thirty-eight cars. Most of this railroad grade can still be seen, but

Tram towers carried the copper ore down to the smelter at Mackay.

little is left of the smelter. In tune with the current upswing in mining, several mines on Mackay Peak are presently active.

MAMMOTH

The breathtaking alpine scenery in Mammoth Canyon must surely have made up for any lack of inspiration the miner received from his diggings. This mining operation was small and only a few cabins were built. Also, there was a small mill that has apparently been destroyed for its scrap metal. An old jeep road leads up the canyon, but it has so many bad spots that you soon end up walking. Surrounded by shale covered ridges with a sprinkling of evergreens in the bottom, the cabins remain in a beautiful setting.

ERA

Far to the southwest of Mackay on Champagne Creek was the small settlement of Era. This town of nearly twelve hundred people blossomed into existence when the Horn Silver Mine was discovered by Frank Martin in 1885. At first the ore was hauled by freight

Limber pines enhance this beautiful setting in Mammoth Basin.

Dry crusher mill at Era was supported by these well built rock foundations.

Miners' cabin on Champagne Creek near Era.

wagons to the smelter in Hailey, but soon a twenty stamp, dry crusher mill was built just south of Era. This mill operated until 1888, when the ore body pinched out, and during these few years Era was at its peak. Like so many mining towns of its day, it had a stage station, a livery stable, three merchandise stores, a drug store, an assay office, dwelling houses, and the usual emporiums for the thirsty. Durable rock foundations are all that remain of the crusher mill, and of the town there is next to nothing. Farther up Champagne Creek there are several other mines with old cabins scattered along the hillsides.

CHAPTER TEN

THE YANKEE FORK AND LOON CREEK

As you travel up the Yankee Fork, a rocky wasteland of dredge tailings follows along the road. With a respite during the war years, when all non-essential mining was closed down, the dredge operated from 1939 until 1952, and at present it is tied up along the road between Bonanza and Custer. When Captain Varney first discovered placer gold near the mouth of Jordan Creek in 1871, he little dreamed of the impact mining would have on the valley. Towns and mills were built, numerous quartz mines were developed, roads

Buildings at the Lucky Boy present a mixture of old and new construction.

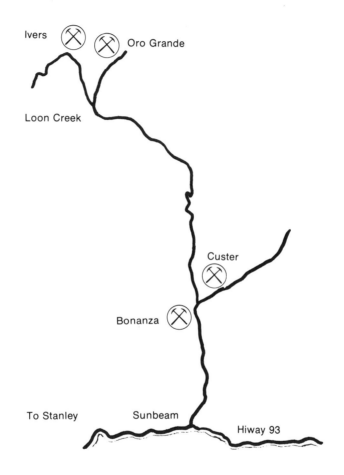

Ivers

Oro Grande

Loon Creek

Custer

Bonanza

To Stanley   Sunbeam

Hiway 93

were hewn out of the mountain sides, and many years later, the banks along the Yankee Fork were churned into barren rock piles. Sunbeam Dam, on the main Salmon River, was built in 1910 to supply electric power for the Golden Sunbeam Mine. Years later this dam was opened up to allow a passageway for the spawning salmon. Farther down the Salmon River, at the mouth of Warm Springs Creek, the guest ranch at Robinson Bar had its origin as an early placer camp.

BONANZA

The rich placers along the Yankee Fork and up Jordan Creek encouraged the miners to build Bonanza City in 1876. By 1880 the town had fifteen hundred people, a post office, stores, hotel, many houses and a newspaper, *The Yankee Herald.* Prior to 1880, Bonanza and Custer were supplied by freighters using pack strings of horses or mules, and the demands of these towns was largely responsible for the growth of Challis as a supply center. Since nearby Custer didn't have a cemetery, the one back in the hills behind Bonanza served both communities. Some log buildings remain along the road in Bonanza, but many have tumbled down and been destroyed.

This dredge piled up the rocky wasteland along the Yankee Fork.

*The McGown museum in Custer is now operated by the
U.S. Forest Service.*

CUSTER

Situated about two miles upstream from Bonanza, Custer grew
with the development of the rich quartz mines. The Charles Dickens
was the first big mine, and others nearby were the General Custer,
the Lucky Boy, the Black Mine, and the Montana Mine. With the
defeat of General Custer in 1876 still fresh in their minds, the miners
named the town in his honor. A toll road over Mill Creek to Challis
was opened in 1880 and allowed freighters to bring in the heavy
machinery that a mill required. The Custer Mill started operating
in 1881 and closed down in 1903, and at one time it had thirty stamps
going. A tramway was built up the mountainside behind the mill
to carry down the ore. Unfortunately the mill has been burned
down and only the foundations remain. Probably the main attraction at Custer is the McGown museum, housed in the old schoolhouse. With the passing of Tuff McGown, the U.S. Forest Service
has taken over the museum.

ORO GRANDE - site

When Nathan Smith discovered placer gold on Loon Creek in

1869, he set off another rush into the back country. Miners have long shown an eagerness for chasing rainbows, and when word of Loon Creek got around, they flocked in from Leesburg, Salmon City, and as far away as Boise Basin. Near the mouth of Canyon Creek, the tent and log town of Oro Grande began to take shape. By 1870 it had a population of fifteen hundred whites and two hundred Chinese, five saloons, stores, a freight office, and many houses. The town was in existence only a short while, and as usual, the Chinese were the last to remain. In 1879 five Chinese miners were killed by Sheepeater Indians. There is some doubt as to whether Indians committed this crime or white men intent on robbing the Chinese of their gold, but the incident helped touch off the Sheepeater Indian War. The townsite was burned over years ago and nothing remains today. The next settler at the mouth of Canyon Creek was Billy Casto, and on most maps, the site of Oro Grande is shown as Casto.

IVERS

In 1902 a young prospector named Clarence Eddy discovered the Lost Packer Mine, and the settlement of Ivers sprang up around the smelter. A road was continued on from Custer, and a hundred

Destructive forest fire left twisted smelter equipment at the Lost Packer Mill in Ivers.

ton smelter was completed in 1905. The town had a store, saloon, several cabins, and about two hundred people. A large forest fire came through this country in 1931, and the mill and part of the town were burned. Some tumbledown cabins remain, however, and the rusting machinery from the mill.

Loon Creek is one of Idaho's more distant areas that is accessible by road, and it presents ever changing vistas of timbered slopes and craggy peaks. A very interesting loop drive can be made by going out the Beaver Creek road from Cape Horn to Pinyon Peak and on down through Ivers to Loon Creek, then back over Loon Creek Summit to Custer. Although passenger cars can make this road, a pickup might prove to be a better vehicle and service stations are nonexistent.

CHAPTER ELEVEN

CHALLIS AREA MINING CAMPS

Challis was founded in 1878 and rapidly grew into a trading center for the many mines nearby. The first settlement, Garden City, was built along the Salmon River at the mouth of Garden Creek. After a very brief life, the town was moved four miles up Garden Creek and renamed after Alvah P. Challis, a pioneer miner and rancher. The completion of the railroad into Blackfoot in 1879 brought the mines closer transportation, but it was still a long haul for the slow moving freight wagons. Mining activity was very high during these years and many people emigrated to the Challis area to work in the mines at Bayhorse, Clayton, and over on the Yankee Fork. Way stations along the toll road from Challis to Custer were operated by Fannie Clark, and along with the always necessary Toll House, these stations were affectionately known to the freighters as Fanny's Upper Hole and Fanny's Lower Hole. Because of its light snowfall, the valley around Challis was used extensively as a wintering ground for the many pack animals then in service.

BAYHORSE

Tim Cooper is credited with finding rich ore up Bayhorse Creek in 1877. The Ramshorn group of mines were among the earliest, others being the Beardsley, the Utah Boy, Idaho, Skylark and Excelsior. In 1880, a five stamp, water powered mill and a twenty-five ton smelter were built. Also, a flume was constructed to carry down the large quantities of wood necessary to charge the kilns. Six charcoal kilns were built, and as they have remained in pretty good condition, they are a favorite with photographers. The operation of a smelter required that large amounts of charcoal be burned to produce the intense heat necessary to melt out the silver and lead. While not the very best fuel, charcoal could be produced locally, whereas coke would have to be freighted in at considerable expense.

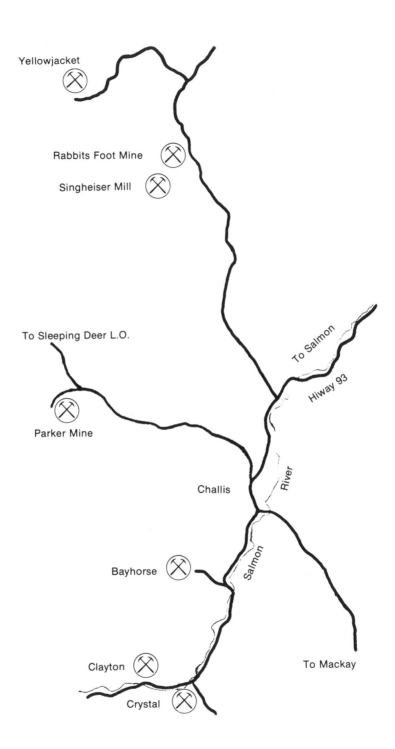

Yellowjacket

Rabbits Foot Mine

Singheiser Mill

To Sleeping Deer L.O.

Parker Mine

To Salmon

Hiway 93

Challis

River

Salmon

Bayhorse

To Mackay

Clayton

Crystal

Hotel at Bayhorse. Rich silver mines at Bayhorse contributed to the growth of Challis.

Three large boilers fed this fallen smokestack at the
Singheiser Mill.

There were other kilns in southern Idaho, notably at Ketchum and Clayton, but these have been destroyed. The mines at Bayhorse are well scattered along the hillsides above the town, with some mining still going on.

CRYSTAL CITY - site

Located at the mouth of the East Fork of the Salmon River, Crystal City in 1884 was one of the largest towns in Custer County. When Custer County was created in 1881 and the location of the county seat was being decided, Crystal lost out to Challis by only three votes. Crystal City had its start as a small freighting settlement when, in 1880, it was the end of the wagon road that came from Ketchum up over Trail Creek to Big Lost River and down Road Creek to the East Fork of the Salmon. Later the road was extended up to Clayton, so that supplies could be freighted into the mines. If you walk out through the sagebrush, you can still see the outlines of buildings and their foundation rocks. Crystal has become little but a memory.

CLAYTON

The mines up Kinnikinik Creek led to the founding of Clayton and the building of a smelter. The Salmon River Mining and Smelting Company operated this smelter in 1881 and 1882, and it ran occasionally doing custom smelting until 1904. Stone foundations and a huge black slag pile down by the river are all that remain of this smelter. The Clayton silver mines are still active, and are some of the oldest mines in Idaho to remain in operation.

YELLOWJACKET

Considered a very lucky prospector by his acquaintances, Nathan Smith is credited with several important mineral discoveries in Idaho. This time, in the fall of 1869, he and "Doc" Wilson discovered placer gold on Yellowjacket Creek. These placer beds led to the development of several quartz mines and the building of the Yellowjacket Mill. The mill was water powered, and the remains of the large wooden flume can be seen along the road. Equipment for the mill was brought in by packstring from Mackay, the heavy iron parts being sectionalized to accommodate the horses. The great-

Huge boardinghouse is dominant feature of Yellowjacket.

Corliss steam engine powered the Singheiser Mill.

est challenge for the pack animals was the heavy cables necessary for the tramway from the mine to the mill. These two cables were a mile long and an inch and a quarter in diameter, and it took eighty pack horses several weeks to haul them in. Quite an accomplishment for the old freighters.

Yellowjacket was in full swing in the 1890s, and even today some mining continues. Many old cabins remain, with the huge five story hotel and boardinghouse the most obvious landmark.

Also to the north of Challis are the Rabbits Foot and the Singheiser mines. These individual mines and mills were large enough to have employed many people. The Singheiser Mill (originally spelled Singiser) was in operation in the early 1900s with a Corliss steam engine running two Joshua Hendy three stamp mills. Bricks were made locally, and this mill has some elaborate brick and stone work. The Parker Mine is north of Challis, off the Sleeping Deer road. This was a smaller venture and very little is left of the mill. The road up past Twin Peaks and out towards Sleeping Deer Lookout gets right up on the skyline and offers a panoramic view of Idaho's rugged Middle Fork Country. Innumerable upthrust peaks traversed by deep, shadowy watercourses present the immensity of Idaho's mountains.

Wooden chutes were used to slide the ore down the steep mountainside to this small crusher at Parker Mountain.

Wooden pulley at the Rabbits Foot Mine. Early machinery was belt driven and most large wheels and pulleys were made of wood.

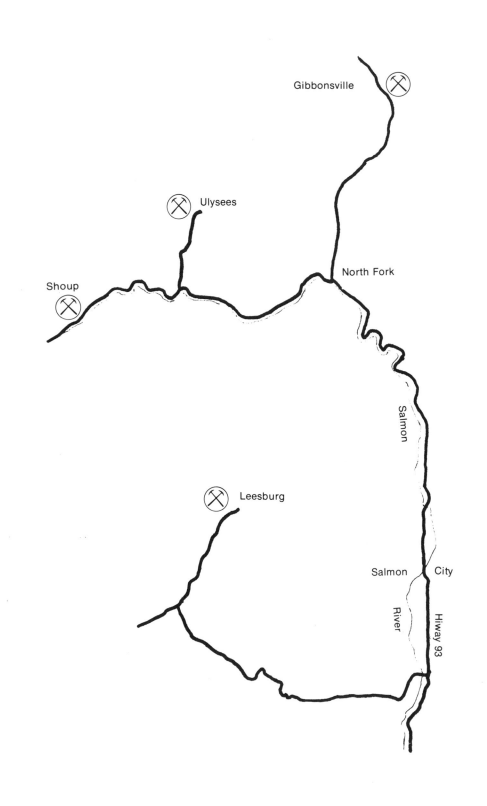

Gibbonsville

Ulysees

Shoup

North Fork

Salmon

Leesburg

Salmon   City

River

Hiway 93

CHAPTER TWELVE

SALMON AREA MINES

Known earlier as Trail City, Salmon City grew out of the need for a supply base for the miners at Leesburg and other surrounding mines. Prior to the development of Salmon, freight had to be packed in from Red Rock, Montana, or north from railheads in Utah. In 1867 Salmon City was laid out by George L. Shoup, who later became Idaho's last Territorial Governor. Besides the major attraction at Leesburg, there were many other mines in the hills around Salmon; Carmen Creek, Kirtley Creek, Bohannon Creek, and Jessie Creek all echoed to the shouts of the miners. High above Salmon near scenic U. P. Lake is the remains of a ten stamp mill that served the Union Pacific and Burlington group of mine claims. To the south of Salmon and up Withington Creek is the huge mill for the Harmony Mine. The Lemhi County Museum in Salmon contains many interesting items from these early mining camps.

LEESBURG

Discovered in 1866 by a party of five miners from Montana, the Leesburg area quickly became the scene of a frantic gold rush. The rows of white miners' tents so filled the meadow that it looked like a field of snow. With a population of three thousand during its prime years, Leesburg was the largest town in Lemhi County. It had close to one hundred businesses, hotels, stores, restaurants, saloons, liveries, and even a newspaper. The main street is quiet now, the old log cabins are starting to lean and come apart, and the noise and excitement of a hundred years ago is only a memory.

During these early mining years, the Civil War was a dominant thought among the miners and resulted in many bitter arguments and barroom brawls. Most of the miners had relatives or friends serving in the armies, and news about the war was eagerly sought after. Even newspapers several weeks old sold quickly at one dollar

The old cabins in Leesburg are token reminders of the booming placer camp of a century ago.

each. Evidence of this North-South split among the miners appeared at Warrens, with the settlements of Richmond and Washington, and at Leesburg, with the camps of Grantsville and Leesburg. In the latter instance the Southern miners chose to name their town Leesburg, while the not-to-be-outdone Northern sympathizers moved their camp a short ways up the road and called it Grantsville. As the camps gradually grew together the name Grantsville lost favor, and Leesburg became the accepted name for the entire community. For all their personal disagreements, both groups sent gold to the same mint, and this great flow of gold into the unionist treasury was extremely beneficial to the Northern cause.

The first mining was mostly placer work along Napias Creek and its many tributaries, but soon the miners spread over into Moose Creek and some turned to quartz mining. The Kirkpatrick Mill was built near Leesburg, and like so many others, it has been destroyed to recover the scrap iron. Up Arnett Creek is the battered remains of the Italian Mill. This huge old mill was a center of activity in the early 1900s, with its three, ten stamp batteries powered by water brought down a long flume. Electric power and lighting was just coming into vogue about this time, and a shed full of broken

*A cable tramway connected the Harmony Mill with ore bins
farther up the mountainside.*

ceramic insulators is testimony that the Italian Mill had electricity.
The huge rock piles along Napias Creek were made in later years
when a washing plant, often called a "doodlebug" by miners, and
a power shovel went down the creek.

The Leesburg area is quite interesting in that there were so
many miners and they literally scoured every stream and gully.
Old cabins pop up here and there, gouges are washed out of hillsides
where some old-timer tried his luck, and the ancient mills just wait
to be photographed. The road on past Leesburg towards Moose
Creek gets pretty rough, and a pickup becomes almost a necessity.
Moose Creek and a tributary, Daly Creek, also saw plenty of action
from the miners. John E. Mullins, a pioneer freighter and rancher
on Moose Creek, hauled in a dredge from Red Rock, Montana, in
1911. As a result of a lawsuit over his freighting bill, Mullins won
control of the boat, and for several years he dredged along Moose
Creek. In an open meadow along Daly Creek was the racetrack,
a reminder of the days when good horseflesh was admired and no
celebration was complete without a race. This three-quarter mile
track was the scene of a race between horses owned by John Mullins
and David McNutt, a wealthy Leesburg mine owner. Much to the

Bricked-up boiler at the Kirkpatrick Mill near Leesburg. Unfortunately, this mill was burned to salvage its scrap iron.

old Scotsman's discomfort, Mullins' horse handily won the race and the fat purse that went with it.

Another small settlement in Leesburg Basin was Smithville. Located farther up Napias Creek at the mouth of Smith's Gulch, it was composed of a store and several cabins. There are no remains. Summit City was a small town on the wagon road from Salmon to Leesburg. It had its start in 1866 and grew to a population of four hundred, but today only the faint outlines of buildings can be seen. With rolling hills well carpeted by lodgepole pine, the Leesburg area is a delightful place to visit.

The following settlements, Gibbonsville, Ulysees, and Shoup, are the three old camps situated north of the Salmon River.

GIBBONSVILLE

Named for Colonel John Gibbons, whose troops engaged Chief Joseph's warriors at the battle of the Big Hole, Gibbonsville had its start in 1877. Placer gold was discovered on Anderson and Dahlonega Creeks, and a short time later quartz prospects led to the building of arrastras and stamp mills. In 1895 the American

The Italian Mill ran in the early 1900s.

*This five stamp Fraser and Chalmers Mill was typical of early
ore crushing machine used in the West.*

Ore bins and the A.D. and M. mine near Gibbonsville.

Development, Mining and Reduction Company constructed a thirty stamp mill and employed six hundred men. Unfortunately there is nothing left of the arrastras and very little left of the old mills. In its early years Gibbonsville was served by roads and trails over the mountains from Montana, and it wasn't until 1889 that Salmon City merchants became interested in promoting a wagon road down the river. Today this demure community along Highway 93 bears little resemblance to the boisterous mining camp of the gay 90s.

ULYSEES

Up Indian Creek from the Salmon River road is the old gold mining settlement of Ulysees. Although claims were located in 1895, it wasn't until 1901 that the Kittie Burton Gold Mining Company acquired the important claims and spurred a burst of activity. With several houses, a large boardinghouse, and the Kittie Burton Mill, it reflected the high hopes of the stockholders. The Kittie Burton Mine was up on a ridge to the west, and the Ulysees mine was high on the east side of the valley. Cable tramways connected both

Wreckage of the Kittie Burton Mill. Tramways from both sides of the valley brought ore to this mill.

Mine buildings border the road below Shoup.

mines with the fifteen stamp mill. The mill was scrapped out and has since collapsed into a shapeless pile, but several houses are still standing.

SHOUP

Better known to the fishermen that frequent the Salmon River, Shoup originated as the town and post office for the Mineral Hill mining district. In the early 1900s the closest road was six miles away, and supplies were floated down the river on barges. The mines were discovered in 1882 with the Grunter and Kentuck being among the first to have stamp mills. Below Shoup and across the river, the old Clipper Bullion Mill can be seen. Shoup is still active today, with vacationers and fishermen taking the place of the old miners.

CHAPTER THIRTEEN

LEADORE - BIRCH CREEK AREA

Junction was the original settlement in the upper Lemhi River Valley and was about a mile and a half east of Leadore. So named because it was at the junction of the Bannock road from Montana and the Mormon wagon road from the south, the town had a hotel, store, several houses, and a population of about two hundred. Northeast of Leadore, the Little Eightmile Mining District had numerous mines, and just east of Leadore, the Leadville Mine was a big producer. The Gilmore and Pittsburgh Railroad was constructed during 1909 and 1910 and ran from Armstead, Montana, through a tunnel under Bannock Pass to Leadore and on to Salmon City. At Armstead, it joined the Utah and Northern Railroad that ran from Butte, Montana, to Logan, Utah. From Leadore, a spur line went on to Gilmore and largely solved the transportation problems that had long handicapped the mines on Texas Creek.

During those years of railroad pioneering it is interesting that in 1909 the Gilmore and Pittsburgh Railroad had a survey crew working down the Salmon River Canyon with the idea of constructing their roadbed on to Lewiston. This railroad, however, was never built, and it is somewhat ironical that just thirty years later, in 1940, the Gilmore and Pittsburgh was authorized to abandon its line from Armstead to Salmon. Today State Highway 28 follows closely along this old roadbed.

GILMORE

Gilmore was named after John T. Gilmer, of the Gilmer and Salisbury Stage Company, but in the process of getting a post office, the spelling was altered. This community can be seen to the west of State Highway 28 and is a mixture of old buildings with those of more recent construction. Like so many mining towns, Gilmore

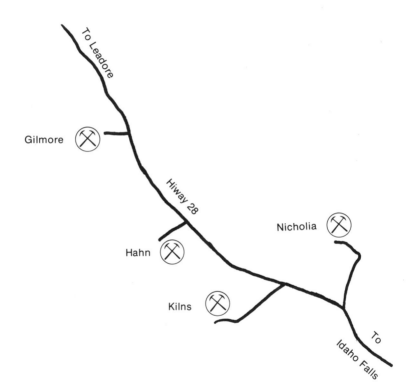

*Charcoal from these kilns was freighted clear across the
valley to the smelter at Nicholia.*

had its spurts of activity mingled with periods of depression, and
this accounts for clusters of log cabins while the store buildings
built later are of sawed lumber.

The discovery of the famous Viola Mine (Nicholia) encouraged
the prospectors to greater efforts, and during the early 1880s, most
of the mines along Texas Creek and Birch Creek were located. In
1902 the Pittsburgh-Idaho group of claims uncovered quality ore
and began freighting it to the railroad at Dubois. The smelter at
Nicholia, which had intermittently served all the smaller mines
in the area, was torn down in 1890, and the railroad hadn't been
started yet, so for four years wagons brought out the ore. The long
haul proved hard on wagons, and during this time steam traction
engines and steel wagons were tried, but finally the company
decided to wait for the railroad. In 1910 the Gilmore and Pittsburgh
Railroad arrived, offering new stimulus to the miners at Gilmore.

HAHN - site

Hahn, with a population of one hundred people, served as the
community center and post office for the many mines on Spring

*Errant breezes drift through rooms that were once lively
with laughter at the hotel in Gilmore.*

Mountain. In 1884, the Spring Mountain Mining Company had a
thirty ton smelter, ore houses, boarding house, and office in Hahn.
A slag pile, cement foundations, and the outlines of buildings are
all that can be seen today.

NICHOLIA

Discovery of the Viola Mine came in 1880, but actual mining
didn't start until 1882, when several car loads of ore were shipped
to Omaha for treatment. In the fall of 1885, a two-stack smelter
was built at the foot of the hills, and the town of Nicholia was
established. In 1886, when only men were permitted to vote, fifteen
hundred men voted at Nicholia. The mine was high on a ridge behind
the town, and a tramway brought the ore down to the smelter.
By looking closely, traces of this old tramway can still be seen.
In later years the slag pile was hauled away to be reworked, so
there is very little to indicate the smelter site.

Perhaps more interesting are the charcoal kilns built to supply
the smelter with fuel and located clear across the valley. It was

This tunnel under Bannock Pass once echoed to the shrill
whistles of the Gilmore and Pittsburgh Railroad.

Rock foundations indicate the old smelter at Hahn.

Nicholia's youngsters learned their three r's in this log building.

necessary to locate the kilns so far away because of a lack of wood and water near the smelter. Of the sixteen kilns constructed, only four remain standing today. Kingville was the settlement for the workers at the kilns, but all the cabins were burned and nothing whatever remains. As you visit this quiet little draw, it is not too difficult to imagine the noise and commotion of yesteryear, teams and wagons bringing in green wood, and clouds of steam and smoke arising from some kilns, while from others the black charcoal was loaded onto wagons for its trip to the smelter. The Targhee Forest has a very interesting self-guided tour among the kilns.

CHAPTER FOURTEEN

CARIBOU DISTRICT

The first placer claims on Mount Pisgah were recorded by F. M. McCoy and F. S. Babcock in 1870. The gold discovery on Barnes Creek soon led to other placers on Anderson Creek, Iowa Creek, Bilk Creek, and McCoy Creek. By 1881 the miners had turned to quartz mining, and three stamp mills were operating. Supplies were freighted in from the railhead at Corinne, Utah, by way of Soda Springs. A miner, nicknamed "Caribou" Jesse Fairchilds, is credited with providing the present-day name to the area.

Miners' camp high in Caribou Basin.

Herman

Keenan
City

Caribou
City

Hiway 34

Wayan

To Soda Springs

KEENAN CITY - site

Keenan City, situated at the confluence of Barnes Creek and City Creek, has the distinction of being the first town in present Bonneville County. The town was built near the site of the original discovery and had a population of five hundred, plus a Chinese community of several hundred. There is ample evidence of early placer mining extending up Barnes Creek for several miles. The remains of several old log cabins can be found here and there up the creek bottom, but at the old townsite there is nothing left.

CARIBOU CITY - site

First known as Iowa Bar or Iowa City, this camp finally settled on the name Caribou City. This was the largest settlement in the area, and with a population of fifteen hundred in 1885, it was a close rival to Eagle Rock (later to become Idaho Falls). The hillsides around Caribou City have been extensively placer mined, with deep gullies gouged into the ground and entire hills washed away. Many

Old prospect shaft required a lot of hard work.

Water was piped long distances to sluice away the
hills around Caribou City.

miles of large metal pipe was used to bring down the water for
the sluice boxes, and this pipe still remains. The quartz mines were
located far above town near the mountain top. As was the fate
of so many mining camps, Caribou City was leveled by fire in 1885
and never rebuilt. The road in becomes quite rough and is barely
passable for a pickup.

CHAPTER FIFTEEN

MISCELLANEOUS MINING CAMPS

These miscellaneous camps are no less interesting or important than any of the other old settlements; it is just that geographically they did not tend to group very well. Quite often it is the more obscure and lesser known mine that is still in nearly original condition. The mills and buildings haven't been broken up and hauled away, so consequently there is much more to photograph. It is most unfortunate that of all the old mines and mills that were in existence so very little has managed to survive. Arrastras could be made simply with materials at hand, and in some areas they were quite numerous. Yet today the remains of arrastras are extremely scarce. Stamp mills contained iron, and while many have been scrapped out, there are still parts and pieces laying around. But a complete battery, with all the iron parts and the wooden frame in good condition, is a rarity. Wood was the most common material in the back country and nearly everything the miners built contained a large share of local timber. Gradually, as the timbers and logs rot away, the only evidence will be scattered, rusty iron and perhaps an old boiler or pulley wheel.

PEARL

Active mines that are closest to Boise are those at Pearl. Although the Consolidated Gem State Mine has been running for many years, renewed interest in mining has created additional activity at Pearl. The hills around town are dotted with old mine dumps and the remnants of buildings. Today just a few people live in Pearl, but at the peak of its mining boom there were many houses strung along the narrow canyon, and the town was as tough as they come.

Once a rip-roaring community, Pearl still has active mines.

NEAL

Another group of mines reasonably close to Boise are those at Neal. These mines, discovered by Arthur Neal in 1889, are located just over the summit from the Upper Blacks Creek Road, formerly known as the Neal Wagon Road. The mine dumps are at the head of the valley, and farther down are a few dilapidated cabins and the skeleton of a mill.

BEAR VALLEY DREDGES

The Bear Valley Dredges are gone. After standing like statues in the open meadow for so many years, they have been dismantled and trucked out of the state. Both as a popular subject for the shutterbug and as a friendly landmark, these huge dredges will be missed by those who travel the road along Bear Valley Creek. The dredges were electrically powered from a generating plant at the camp on the east side of the valley, and the rare metals they sought were Columbium, Tantalum and Monazite. Another dredge

Frame of old stamp mill at Neal.

Both dredges in Bear Valley were dismantled and hauled away in 1969 and 1970. This was the larger of the pair.

*Deadwood City was one early camp that died and was brought
back to life with improved mining methods.*

that may still be seen is the one on Big Creek, a few miles south
of Cascade.

DEADWOOD CITY

This old mining camp on the upper Deadwood River was located
near the present Deadwood Lodge. Back against the hills behind
the Lodge are the remains of the mine buildings, and the tailings
pile extends clear out to the road. Lead, silver, and gold were the
metals sought after, and several old cabins are scattered along the
road below the Lodge. Started in 1867, the first settlement only
lasted about seven or eight years, but periodic bursts of activity
continued over the years, with the latest occurring in the early
1940s.

THE MARY JANE and THE MARY BLUE MINES

These two old mines are also in the Deadwood area. The old
mill at the Mary Jane has been demolished, but a few cabins have
survived. Scattered out under the evergreens are many rotting piles

of cordwood that were cut to fire the boiler and never used. A few buildings remain at the Mary Blue Mine.

CEDARVILLE - site

North of Howe and up South Creek from Little Lost River was the small community of Cedarville. Mining was carried on up South Creek and in nearby North Creek, with the Daisy Black or Wilbert claim being the largest producer. Only scattered rocks from the foundations mark this townsite.

TWIN SPRINGS

All up and down the Middle Fork of the Boise River are the rockpiles and gullies washed out by placer mining. Much of this was done by hydraulic giants, a method of placer mining in which a powerful stream of water is directed into a hillside and washes the sand and gravel down through long sluice boxes. Miles of expensive flumes were built along the hills above the Boise River, and near Twin Springs a bridge was built to carry the flume across

This boiler once ran a jaw crusher at the Mary Jane mine.

the river to rich placer ground. This activity occurred about 1900, and Twin Springs was the leading settlement for the miners and their "giants."

SNAKE RIVER CAMPS

Placer gold was found along the Snake River from Eagle Rock (Idaho Falls) on down. This gold was very fine and difficult to catch in a sluice box, so many novel methods of trapping the golden particles were tried. In the early 1870s the placer camps of Springtown, Mudbarville, Dry Town, and Waterburg were going strong. Springtown was on the south bank of the Snake River, one-half mile below the Hansen Bridge, Mudbarville was at the mouth of Mud Creek, northwest of Buhl, and Dry Town was at the mouth of Dry Creek, near Murtaugh. Many other individual claims are scattered down the river, with some gouging being done along the river bank south of Melba.

Giant nozzles, like this small one, were used to direct the stream of water into the hillside and wash out the gold bearing gravel.

SEAFOAM MINE

Far to the north of the Stanley to Lowman highway is the remote Seafoam mining area. The road in passes through the tiny settlement of Wagon Town, recently marked with a Forest Service historical sign. Wagon Town served as a way station for the freighters plying between the Greyhound Mine and Challis. With numerous streams and high mountain lakes accessible by trail only, this portion of scenic Idaho is probably better known to the dedicated fisherman. Discovered in 1886, the mines were predominately lead and silver. The mill building still stands at the Seafoam Mine, as do several other large buildings. The road in is barely passable with a pickup, and a four-wheel drive rig would be much better.

GREYHOUND MINE

Another well known mine in the Seafoam District is the Greyhound. The ten stamp mill was steam powered and a small smelter was built. Freighting boilers and other heavy equipment

*Wagon Town echoed to the shouts of the freighters plying
between the Greyhound Mine and Challis.*

Mill at Seafoam Mine is slowly falling apart.

over such tortuous country must have caused many a freighter to shift his chew and address his team with a string of well chosen words. To judge from the huge, rotting pile of logs stacked near the boiler room, someone many years ago certainly didn't intend to run out of firewood. Log ore bins and several cabins are still standing.

The old mines and mills presented here are by no means all that can be found in the southern half of Idaho, but they are fairly representative of the many mining districts that abound, and most of the larger and better known settlements are included. Whether your interest lies in history, photography, bottle collecting, or in just getting outdoors, the old mining communities offer something special to everyone. The pictures in this book show only a small part: there is much more to see, other places to visit, and any number of subjects to entice the photographer. But perhaps best of all, the old camps extend an invitation to enjoy the beauty and quiet to be found in Idaho's magnificent mountains, and to share, if only briefly, in the lives of our early day miners.

*Silver and lead discoveries in 1886 spurred the development
of the Seafoam Mine.*

Steep, timbered slopes surround the Greyhound Mill.